Breaking the Chain: Cutting Toxic Family Ties and Reclaiming Your Life

By

Stacie Webb

Paperback: 9798893978117

Hardcover: 9798893978124

Dedication

To everyone who has ever been told they are "too sensitive" for wanting to be treated with dignity, you were right to trust your feelings. To those who chose their well-being over family expectations and said "no more" when everyone else said "but they're family"; your courage breaks toxic cycles for generations you'll never meet. And to the readers holding this book, wondering if they have the right to want something different, you do, you always have, and you are worth fighting for.

About the Author

Stacie is a survivor, advocate, and author who understands the profound courage it takes to choose healing over family loyalty. After years of enduring toxic family dynamics, she made the difficult decision to cut ties with her entire family of origin, a choice that ultimately saved her life and allowed her to build the authentic, loving relationships she had always deserved.

With a background in the medical field, Stacie was forced to step away from her healthcare career due to health challenges that were, in part, connected to the long-term effects of family trauma. This transition became an unexpected gift, leading her to discover that writing could be a powerful way to help others navigate similar journeys.

Breaking the Chain: Cutting Toxic Family Ties and Reclaiming Your Life is Stacie's first book, born from her own lived experience and the realization that too many people suffer in silence, believing she had no choice but to endure toxic family relationships. Through extensive research and her own healing journey, she has created a comprehensive guide for others facing these impossible decisions.

Stacie's approach combines hard-won personal wisdom with carefully researched insights from psychology, trauma recovery, and family systems theory. Having walked this path herself, from recognizing toxic patterns to setting boundaries, going no contact, grieving what never was, and ultimately building a chosen family, she writes with the authenticity that can only come from lived experience.

The process of writing this book became an integral part of Stacie's own healing journey. Each chapter written was another step toward processing her experiences, understanding the broader patterns of family dysfunction, and transforming personal pain into something that could serve others. She discovered that helping others find their way to safety and healing has become not just her passion, but her purpose.

Today, Stacie lives surrounded by her chosen family; people who demonstrate daily what healthy love actually looks like. She is passionate about normalizing conversations around family estrangement, challenging cultural myths about unconditional family loyalty, and supporting others who are questioning relationships that others might never examine.

Stacie believes deeply that healing is possible for everyone, even when it feels impossible. She understands that sometimes the most loving thing you can do for yourself and future generations is to break the cycle of dysfunction that has been passed down through your family line. This understanding began early for Stacie; even as a middle schooler, she made a promise to herself that when she grew up and had children of her own, she would figure out a way to break the toxic patterns she was witnessing at home. That young girl's determination to create something different became the driving force behind her adult journey toward healing and ultimately inspired her to write this book, hoping to help others find their own path to breaking generational cycles of harm.

When not writing, Stacie enjoys hanging out with her dogs, playing games, listening to music, watching TV, hanging out with her chosen family, and ultimately still continues her own healing work, knowing that recovery is not a destination but an ongoing journey of growth, self-discovery, self-love, and authentic living.

"My hope is that this book reaches people who need to know they're not alone in questioning family relationships that others might never examine. Every person deserves to feel safe, valued, and genuinely loved in their most important relationships. If your family of origin cannot provide that, you have every right, and often the necessity, to create a chosen family that can."

"Writing this book saved me as much as I hope it will save others. Sometimes we have to break completely before we can rebuild ourselves into who we were always meant to be. Your healing journey is valid, your choices are brave, and you are worth fighting for."

— Stacie Webb

Acknowledgments

Writing a book about cutting toxic family ties feels both deeply personal and profoundly universal. This work exists because countless individuals have had the courage to break the silence, question harmful patterns, and choose healing over familiar dysfunction. To everyone who has shared their story, sought support, or simply dared to imagine that their family relationships could be different, this book is for you and because of you.

To the Survivors and Thrivers

First and foremost, I want to acknowledge the thousands of individuals who have shared their experiences in support groups, online communities, therapy sessions, and private conversations. Your stories, marked by both profound pain and extraordinary resilience, have shaped every page of this book. To those who found the courage to say "no more" to relationships that diminished them, who chose their well-being over family expectations, and who built new definitions of love and loyalty, you are the true authors of this work.

To the members of online communities like the countless Facebook support groups where people find their voices and their people, thank you for creating spaces where truth-telling is not only allowed but celebrated. The lessons I've learned from you are woven into every chapter, and your mutual support demonstrates daily what a healthy family actually looks like.

To My Faithful Companions

To my dogs, both past and present, Jodie, Pip, Snoopy, Sadie, Gibbs, Missy, Chaquita, Buddy, and Ducky, who have been my most consistent source of unconditional love. When human relationships felt unsafe or impossible, you were there to lick away my tears, offer silent snuggles when the world felt too heavy, and provide comfort when I felt I had nowhere else to turn. You taught me what love without conditions actually looks like, and your presence during my darkest moments reminded me that I was worthy of gentle, consistent care. In many ways, you were my first chosen family, showing me that love is about showing up, not about blood or obligation.

To the Mental Health Professionals

I am deeply grateful to the therapists, researchers, and clinicians whose dedication to understanding family trauma has not only shaped this book but has also been a guiding light in my own healing journey.

To the countless therapists who sit with survivors week after week, validating experiences that families denied, and helping people rebuild their sense of self from the ground up, your work saves lives in ways that cannot be measured. To those who have specialized in treating narcissistic abuse, family estrangement, and complex trauma, thank you for choosing to work in spaces where healing is possible but never simple.

To the Researchers and Writers

Gratitude to the academic researchers who have legitimized family estrangement as a field worthy of serious study. Your research has provided the evidence base that validates what survivors have always known; sometimes leaving is the healthiest choice.

To the authors who wrote the books that changed lives before this one existed, thank you for being willing to name what others preferred to keep hidden. Your courage to write difficult truths paved the way for conversations that are now saving generations.

To Those Who Choose to Understand

To the friends, partners, and chosen family members who have stood by people making the difficult choice to limit contact with toxic family members, your support has been literally life-saving. In a world that often pressures people to "forgive and forget," you have offered something more valuable: the understanding that love sometimes means protecting yourself from those who cannot love you safely.

To the therapists, doctors, teachers, and community members who, when someone says "my family is complicated," respond with curiosity rather than judgment, thank you for creating the emotional safety that makes healing possible.

To the Community Builders

This book exists because of people who built communities where none existed before. To the online moderators who maintain safe spaces for difficult conversations, the support group facilitators who hold space for both grief and growth, and the individuals who show up consistently for others even while doing their own healing work, you have created the villages that raise healthy adults from wounded children.

To those who model what a chosen family can look like, who celebrate birthdays and provide emergency support, who remember the small things and show up for the big things, you demonstrate daily that DNA is not destiny and that love is always a choice.

To the Professional Community

To my editors, who helped shape raw emotion into something that could serve others. To the sensitivity readers who ensured this work honored the complexity of family estrangement without oversimplifying or causing additional harm. To the legal and ethical consultants who helped navigate the careful balance between sharing wisdom and protecting privacy.

To Those Who Are Still Deciding

To readers who picked up this book while still in a relationship with toxic family members, uncertain about what boundaries to set or whether estrangement might be necessary, your courage to even consider these questions deserves recognition. Questioning family dynamics that others accept without examination takes extraordinary strength.

To those who are in the early stages of setting boundaries or have recently gone no contact, the path you're walking is difficult, but you are not walking it alone. Every person who has walked this path before you is cheering you on.

To the Future

To the children who will grow up in healthier families because someone broke the cycle. To the adults who will never have to question their worth because they were raised by people who did their own healing work. To the communities that will be strengthened by individuals who learned to love themselves enough to choose relationships that nourish rather than deplete them.

To the researchers who will continue studying family estrangement and developing better interventions. To the therapists who will be trained in trauma-informed approaches to family dysfunction. To the writers who will continue giving language to experiences that need to be named and normalized.

Personal Acknowledgments

To my own chosen family and friends, Celia, Pam, Mai Ling, Nora, Tamra, Nevaeh, Raianna, Shawn, Renee, Saia, Jaden, and countless others, the very people who have shown me what healthy love looks like and supported my healing journey even when it was messy and nonlinear. You have taught me that family is not about perfection but about showing up consistently with genuine love, care, and respect. You have modeled how to hold space for others' pain without being consumed by it.

To my own past therapists and current healers who have guided me through my own family-of-origin work and who have shown me that healing is possible even when it feels impossible.

A Special Recognition

To the readers to those we cannot name because their stories are still too dangerous to tell publicly, the individuals who must maintain family relationships for safety, financial, or legal reasons, while doing internal work to protect their well-being. Your healing matters too, and your strategies for survival in impossible situations deserve recognition and support.

To those who did not survive, who were lost to suicide, addiction, or other consequences of family trauma before they could find the support they needed. Your lives mattered, your pain was real, and your loss drives us to do better for those who come after.

To the Readers

Finally, to those who are reading this book, whether you found it in crisis or curiosity, whether you're just beginning to question family patterns or are years into your healing journey, thank you for having the courage to consider that your well-being matters enough to examine these relationships seriously.

You deserve love that doesn't require you to hide parts of yourself. You deserve relationships where your feelings are met with empathy rather than dismissal. You deserve to feel safe in your most important connections. If your family of origin cannot provide these things, you have the right to find or create a family that can.

This book exists because you deserve to know that choosing yourself is not selfish; it's necessary. You are worth the difficult work of breaking toxic patterns and building authentic relationships. You are worth the courage it takes to live according to your values rather than others' expectations.

Your healing journey, whatever it looks like, is valid and valuable. You are not alone.

The work of breaking toxic family cycles and building healthy relationships is never done alone. It is community work, healing work, and legacy work. Thank you to everyone who has contributed to making this book possible, and to everyone who will carry its message forward.

May we continue to build a world where every person knows their inherent worth and has access to relationships that honor their full humanity.

— Stacie Webb

Table of Contents

Introduction

I wrote this book because I've been through it—the heartbreak, the confusion, and the isolation that comes from cutting ties with toxic family members. This is not a path I ever imagined taking, but it became absolutely necessary for my survival, my healing, and my growth. If you've picked up this book, you're likely standing at a similar crossroads—or maybe you've already taken that brave first step.

This book is a companion for those navigating the painful and often misunderstood experience of separating from toxic family dynamics. Whether you're in the early stages of questioning your reality or years into your healing journey, this book was written to validate, support, and empower you.

Cutting ties with a family member—or your entire family, goes against almost every message we're taught about loyalty and love. Society tells us that family is everything. But what happens when that "everything" comes at the cost of your well-being, your peace, or your identity??

In the pages that follow, you'll find practical guidance, emotional support, and reflective exercises designed to help you:

- Understand toxic family dynamics and how they impact your sense of self
- Release guilt, shame, and obligation that's been unfairly placed on you
- Set and enforce boundaries without apology
- Grieve the relationship you deserved but never had
- Reclaim your worth and build a life that aligns with your truth

This isn't a book about revenge or bitterness. It's a book about liberation. About reclaiming your right to peace. And it's for anyone who has ever stayed silent to keep the peace—only to realize that silence was breaking them instead.

You are not alone. Your pain is real. And your healing matters.

Before we dive in, grab a notebook or journal to use for the Reflection Prompts & Healing Journal Practice sections throughout this book. Writing your thoughts can deepen your healing journey and provide clarity as you work through each chapter.

Let's begin.

Chapter 1: Understanding Toxic Family Dynamics

The word "toxic" has become commonplace in our conversations about relationships, but when applied to family, it carries a weight that can feel almost impossible to bear. Toxic or dysfunctional family dynamics can be hard to recognize, especially when you're still entrenched in them. For many of us, the very people who were supposed to provide love, safety, and support became sources of confusion, pain, and emotional chaos.

Understanding what makes a family toxic isn't about assigning blame or creating enemies out of the people who raised us. It's about developing the clarity needed to protect ourselves and make informed decisions about our relationships. Mental health professionals emphasize the importance of recognizing and addressing these patterns—not only to protect yourself from long-term psychological harm, but also to break the cycle of toxicity and support healing.

What Makes a Family Toxic?

All families struggle from time to time, but the family members still feel loved, supported, and respected. A toxic or dysfunctional family dynamic, on the other hand, can feel unstable, tense, and charged. Toxic family members can cause a great deal of harm. The difference lies not in the presence of conflict—all families have disagreements—but in the patterns of how conflict is handled, how power is distributed, and whether family members feel safe to be themselves.

Toxic families operate under fundamentally different rules than healthy ones. In healthy families, love is unconditional, mistakes are learning opportunities, and individual growth is celebrated. Secure and supportive family relationships provide love, advice, and care. Stressful family relationships are often marked by arguments, relentless criticism, and overwhelming demands.

In toxic families, love becomes conditional—something to be earned through compliance, achievement, or playing specific roles. Toxic families or toxic family members may make you feel bad about yourself, your accomplishments, or your life overall. They may do this covertly or overtly, but after you spend time with a toxic family member, you are most likely to feel more down on yourself than you did before seeing them.

The toxicity often manifests through:

- *Control disguised as care:* "I'm only doing this because I love you" becomes the justification for invasive, controlling behavior.
- *Emotional manipulation:* Guilt, shame, and fear become tools for getting compliance.
- *Conditional acceptance:* Love and approval are withdrawn when you don't meet expectations.
- *Boundary violations:* Your privacy, autonomy, and individual needs are consistently dismissed.
- *Role rigidity:* Family members are locked into specific roles that serve the dysfunction rather than their individual growth.

Common Patterns and Behaviors

Toxic behaviors often manifest through subtle manipulation, constant criticism, and intense jealousy, creating an environment of emotional instability. These patterns can be difficult to identify because they often develop gradually and become normalized within the family system.

The Accountability Vacuum

The inability to take any kind of accountability is one big sign of toxicity. A parent, sibling, or other family member may often place blame for anything that's wrong on someone else—you, included. In toxic families, someone else is always at fault. The toxic family member positions themselves as the perpetual victim, unable to see their role in family problems.

Emotional Manipulation as Love Language

If someone is toxic, you can bet they're going to be manipulative, which can look like a lot of different things. They may gaslight you, guilt-trip you, or be controlling in general. Another characteristic of a toxic individual in a family is a family member being manipulative or making you feel guilty or bad for not doing something.

The Silent Treatment as Punishment

Adults in toxic relationships often use the silent treatment as a form of punishment. This emotional withdrawal is designed to make you feel desperate for reconnection, often leading you to apologize or comply even when you've done nothing wrong.

Boundary Violations as Normal

Zero boundaries between family members – being close is one thing, but healthy relationships also have a sense of autonomy. Examples of lack of boundaries: having no personal space, family members walking into your room and going through your personal things, reading diaries, listening in to phone calls.

Triangulation and Drama Creation

Indirect communication – in dysfunctional families, information, news, or gossip tends to get spread in an indirect manner via other family members. Rather than addressing conflicts directly, toxic family members involve third parties, create alliances, and use others to deliver their messages.

Why It's Hard to See Clearly from the Inside

As children, we don't always have the ability to identify right from wrong, and healthy or unhealthy behaviour. Because of this, if a child grows up around toxic behaviour, they're likely to either normalise it or internalise it by believing it's their fault – and often both.

When you grow up in dysfunction, it becomes your normal. Many people don't realize the effects of their family environment during childhood until they're well into adulthood. The toxic patterns feel familiar, and familiar often feels like love, even when it's actually harmful.

Factors that can make it difficult to recognize the toxicity from within include:

The Survival Brain Takes Over

This results in deep fear of abandonment. As adults, any kind of distance, even a brief and benign one, may trigger you to re-experience the original pain of being left alone, dismissed, or disdained. Your fear could trigger coping survival modes such as denial, clinging, avoidance, dismissing others, lashing out in relationships, or the pattern of sabotaging relationships to avoid potential rejection.

Gaslighting Creates Self-Doubt

When your reality is consistently questioned, dismissed, or rewritten by family members, you learn not to trust your own perceptions. You start to question whether your feelings are valid, whether your memories are accurate, and whether you're being "too sensitive."

The Fantasy Family Lives in Your Heart

Most people hold onto hope that their family relationships will eventually become what they've always wanted them to be. This hope can be so powerful that it prevents you from seeing the relationship as it actually is, rather than as you wish it could be.

Cultural and Social Conditioning

Society reinforces the idea that "family is everything" and that we must honor our parents and maintain family unity regardless of the cost to our own well-being. Abusive relationships should never be tolerated – family or otherwise.

Physical and Emotional Responses

If you've experienced a toxic family dynamic, your feelings may go beyond frustration or annoyance. Instead, interacting with or even thinking about your family might cause significant emotional distress. Physical symptoms can appear, such as: feeling drained, back and neck pain, jaw-clenching, digestive troubles or a tightness in your stomach.

Your body often knows before your mind does. Pay attention to how you feel before, during, and after family interactions. Anxiety, depression, physical tension, or a sense of dread can all be signals that something is wrong.

The Long-Term Impact

The impact of prolonged exposure to toxic family dynamics extends beyond emotional well-being, potentially manifesting in physical health issues and increased vulnerability to domestic violence in future relationships. Unhealthy family dynamics can cause children to experience trauma and stress as they grow up. This type of exposure, famously known as adverse childhood experiences (ACEs), is linked to an increased risk of developing physical and mental health problems. Specifically, ACEs increase an individual's risk of developing heart, lung, or liver disease, depression, anxiety, and more.

The effects ripple through all areas of life:

- *Relationships:* You have a pattern of troubled romantic relationships – children from dysfunctional families will often end up playing out these unhealthy dynamics in later life – either from a subconscious desire to "fix" the dysfunction they encountered in childhood or because it feels familiar.

- *Self-Worth:* Dysfunctional family dynamics can warp your whole sense of self-worth. Growing up in dysfunction and continuing to live in it, it can feed these beliefs that you aren't good enough, or that people don't really love or care for you and never will.
- *Identity Formation:* Toxic family dynamics significantly impact self-esteem and identity formation, often leading to long-lasting effects on confidence and self-worth. Individuals raised in such environments may struggle with code-pendency issues, constantly seeking validation from others, and having difficulty establishing a strong sense of self.

Reflection Prompts & Healing Journal Practice

Take some time with these questions. There's no rush—healing happens at its own pace, and awareness is the first step toward freedom.

Understanding Your Family System:

1. When you think about your childhood home, what comes to mind to describe the emotional atmosphere?
2. Were you allowed to express all your emotions (anger, sadness, disappointment) or only positive ones?
3. How were conflicts handled in your family? Were they resolved, or did they simmer under the surface?
4. What happened when you tried to set boundaries or say no?
5. Did you feel safe to be yourself, or did you learn to perform a specific role to maintain peace?

Recognizing Patterns:

1. What physical sensations do you notice when you think about spending time with your family?
2. How do you typically feel after family interactions—energized or drained?
3. What topics are off-limits in your family conversations?
4. When you achieve something positive, how does your family usually respond?
5. Are you able to disagree with family members without facing retaliation?

Your Body's Wisdom:

1. Pay attention to your body for the next week. Notice any changes in how you feel when:

   - You see your family's name on your phone
   - You're preparing to visit or call them
   - You're in their physical presence
   - You're driving home after seeing them

2. Keep a simple log: Rate your energy and mood on a scale of 1-10 before and after family contact. Notice patterns.

Healing Affirmations to Practice:

   - "My feelings and perceptions are valid."
   - "I deserve to be treated with respect and kindness."
   - "It's not my job to manage other people's emotions."
   - "I can love someone and still protect myself from their harmful behavior."
   - "Recognizing toxicity doesn't make me disloyal—it makes me healthy."

Recognizing toxic family dynamics isn't about becoming bitter or resentful. Healing means moving beyond the rules that govern dysfunctional family dynamics. You can replace don't talk, don't trust, don't feel with a new set of guidelines in your adult relationships. You can break down shame, isolation, and loneliness, and build more connected relationships when you share your thoughts and feelings with trustworthy people. Acknowledging and talking about your problems is the opposite of staying in denial. It opens the door to solutions and healing.

This chapter is about developing the clarity and self-awareness needed to make informed decisions about your relationships. You deserve to surround yourself with people who support your growth, respect your boundaries, and celebrate your authentic self. Understanding what you've experienced is the first step toward reclaiming your life.

Chapter 2: Guilt, Obligation, and the Invisible Contracts We Inherit

"Guilt is anger directed at ourselves — at what we did or did not do. Resentment is anger directed at others — at what they did or did not do." — Peter McWilliams

The weight of family guilt can feel heavier than a physical burden, pressing down on your chest every time you consider prioritizing your own needs. It whispers in the quiet moments: "You're being selfish." "After everything they've done for you." "What kind of person abandons their family?" This guilt didn't appear overnight—it was carefully cultivated, passed down through generations like a toxic heirloom, and woven so deeply into the fabric of your identity that you may not even recognize it as separate from love.

Understanding how guilt operates as a tool of control in toxic family systems is crucial to breaking free from the invisible contracts that bind you to relationships that harm rather than heal.

How Guilt Is Used to Control

Guilt is perhaps one of the most powerful weapons in a toxic family member's arsenal because it exploits the natural human desire to avoid feelings of guilt and can be used to elicit compliance in others. Unlike other forms of manipulation that might be obvious or aggressive, guilt operates in the shadows, disguised as love, concern, or family loyalty.

People often use guilt to try to get you to take responsibility for something that isn't your fault. When you feel guilty, you're more likely to do what the other person wants. This includes trying to resolve the problem for them. In toxic families, this becomes a systematic pattern where your natural empathy and desire to maintain relationships are turned against you.

The Anatomy of Family Guilt Trips

Toxic family members are masters of the subtle guilt trip. They've learned exactly which buttons to push to activate your compliance, often using phrases that sound loving but carry a manipulative undertone, such as:

- "I guess I'm just a terrible mother/father." (When you try to set a boundary)

- "After everything I've sacrificed for this family..." (When you make a choice they disagree with)
- "I don't ask for much." (Right before asking for everything)
- "You're the only one who really understands me." (Creating false specialness and obligation)
- "If you really loved me, you would..." (Making love conditional on compliance)
- "I know I wasn't a great parent, but..." (Deflecting responsibility and silencing your pain)
- "I'm just in the 'fake it till you make it' stage of life." (A way of dodging accountability and refusing to engage in the hard, vulnerable work of repairing the relationship.)

Instead of choosing honesty, self-reflection, or meaningful effort with their adult child, they hide behind performance — leaving the burden of healing on the child. These are tactics that look like self-criticism on the surface, but really, they're tactics to shut down your truth, invalidate your experience, and avoid accountability.

Individuals who remind you of all they've done for you—a laundry list of their superiority—could be using that as manipulation, a reminder that you should feel guilty for not measuring up. Remarks like "I'm the one who cares the most" or "I've always done that for you" are leading statements meant to provoke negative feelings of guilt in others—and get them to give in.

The "Sacrificial Narrative"

One of the most insidious forms of guilt manipulation involves the constant reminder of sacrifices made. Toxic parents, in particular, excel at this tactic. Manipulators keep a checklist of the favors they believe others owe them and never engage in positive behaviors without ulterior motives. If a chronic manipulator has offered to help you in some way, you can be certain they will call that in as a favor down the road. In fact, many times, they help without being asked—or even after being asked not to help—just to gain a sense of one-upmanship in the relationship.

The message becomes clear: your existence has cost them something, and you owe them perpetual gratitude and compliance. This creates what psychologists call "toxic guilt"—when other people manipulate you with guilt or put their emotional baggage on you.

Emotional Blackmail and Threats

When subtle guilt doesn't work, toxic family members often escalate to more overt emotional blackmail. Some other forms of guilt-tripping could be blackmailing us by using our sense of shame or guilt, or the manipulator harming themselves so that we agree to their demands. This might include:

- Threats of self-harm if you don't comply
- Playing the victim to avoid accountability
- Using other family members as weapons ("Your grandmother will be so disappointed")
- Threatening to disown or abandon you
- Creating medical or emotional "emergencies" that require your immediate attention

Distinguishing Love from Obligation

One of the most challenging aspects of toxic family relationships is learning to distinguish between genuine love and manufactured obligation. Toxic families excel at conflating the two, creating a belief system where love must be earned through compliance and sacrifice.

What Real Love Looks Like

Healthy family love is:

- *Unconditional:* It doesn't disappear when you make choices others disagree with
- *Supportive:* It celebrates your growth and independence
- *Respectful:* It honors your boundaries and individual needs
- *Consistent:* It doesn't fluctuate based on your behavior or compliance
- *Empowering:* It encourages you to become your authentic self

What Obligation Disguised as Love Looks Like

Toxic obligation masquerading as love is:

- *Conditional:* "I'll love you if you do what I want"
- *Controlling:* Your choices must align with family expectations
- *Guilt-driven:* Love is withdrawn as punishment for non-compliance
- *Sacrificial:* You must continually prove your worthiness through sacrifice

- *Limiting:* It discourages growth that threatens the family system

A common sign of manipulation in relationships is when you start losing a sense of who you are after following someone else's overt or covert demands to give up your opinions and interests. In family relationships, it may be that you don't feel you can fully express who you are as a person and your life choices, and you may act differently when you're around them.

Breaking Unspoken Family Roles

Every family system assigns roles to its members, often without anyone consciously choosing them. In toxic families, these roles become rigid prisons that serve the dysfunction rather than the individuals within the system. Breaking free from these inherited roles is essential to reclaiming your authentic identity.

The Common Toxic Family Roles

The Scapegoat: You're blamed for the family's problems and bear the brunt of criticism and anger. Your role is to absorb the family's dysfunction and provide a target for their collective rage and disappointment.

The Golden Child: You're praised and favored, but only as long as you maintain the family's image and meet impossible expectations. Your worth is tied to your achievements and ability to make the family look good.

The Lost Child: You disappear into the background, avoiding conflict by becoming invisible. Your needs are consistently overlooked because you don't cause problems.

The Caretaker: You're responsible for everyone else's emotional well-being. Your role is to fix, heal, and manage other people's feelings at the expense of your own.

The Mascot: You use humor and entertainment to deflect tension and maintain family cohesion. Your authentic emotions are hidden behind a performative facade.

The Mediator: You're constantly trying to keep the peace, smoothing over conflicts and managing everyone else's relationships with each other.

It is not uncommon to be put into several toxic family roles, as I was.

The Cost of Playing These Roles

These roles come with invisible contracts—unspoken agreements about what you owe the family system in exchange for belonging. The cost includes:

- *Loss of authentic identity*: You become so focused on your role that you lose touch with who you really are
- *Emotional exhaustion*: Managing everyone else's needs leaves no energy for your own
- *Stunted development*: You can't grow beyond the role the family needs you to play
- *Relationship difficulties*: The patterns you learn in your family role follow you into other relationships
- *Mental health challenges*: The pressure to maintain these roles can lead to anxiety, depression, and identity confusion

The Invisible Contracts

Toxic families operate on a system of invisible contracts—unspoken agreements about what each family member owes the others. These contracts are never explicitly negotiated, but the consequences for breaking them are severe.

Common invisible contracts include:

- "You will always put family first, regardless of the cost to yourself"
- "You will not discuss family problems with outsiders"
- "You will maintain the family image, even if it means lying"
- "You will sacrifice your own needs to meet the needs of other family members"
- "You will not change or grow in ways that threaten the family system"
- "You will accept poor treatment because 'that's just how family is'"

The insidious nature of these contracts is that you never actually agreed to them—they were imposed upon you through guilt, manipulation, and the threat of losing your place in the family.

Guided Reflection: Releasing Guilt and Rewriting the Narrative

The journey to freedom begins with recognizing these patterns and consciously choosing to rewrite the stories you've been told about love, loyalty, and obligation. The following exercises will help you identify the guilt patterns in your life and begin the process of liberation.

Reflection Questions

Take time to journal on these questions, allowing yourself to write freely without judgment:

1. *Identifying Guilt Patterns:*

   o What situations or requests from family members trigger immediate guilt in you?

   o What phrases or words do your family members use that make you feel instantly responsible or obligated?

   o Can you identify specific moments when guilt was used to change your behavior or decisions?

2. *Recognizing Your Family Role:*

   o Which of the family roles described above resonates most with your experience?

   o How has this role limited your growth or authentic self-expression?

   o What would happen if you stopped playing this role? What are you most afraid of?

3. *Distinguishing Love from Obligation:*

   o Think of a time when you felt genuinely loved versus a time when you felt obligated. What was different about these experiences?

   o When you imagine disappointing a family member, what do you fear losing? Is it love or approval?

   o How do you show love to others? Is it similar to how your family shows "love" to you?

The Guilt Audit Exercise

Create three columns on a piece of paper. Don't overthink this!

Column 1: The Guilt Trigger

List the situations, requests, or conversations that make you feel guilty regarding family relationships.

Column 2: The Underlying Message

For each trigger, identify the underlying message. What is the guilt trying to make you believe about yourself or your obligations?

Column 3: The Reality Check

Challenge each message with facts. Is this guilt based on something you actually did wrong, or is it manufactured to control your behavior?

Rewriting Your Narrative Exercise

Step 1: Write down the story your family tells about you. This might include labels like "the selfish one," "the ungrateful one," "the one who never calls," etc.

Step 2: Write down the story you want to tell about yourself. Who are you when you're not defined by your family role? What are your values, dreams, and authentic characteristics?

Step 3: Create bridge statements that help you transition from the old narrative to the new one:

- "I am learning that self-care is not selfish"
- "I can love my family and still set boundaries"
- "My worth is not determined by how much I sacrifice"
- "I have the right to make choices that support my well-being"
- "I have the right to live life on my own terms"

The Permission Letter

Write a letter to yourself giving yourself permission to release guilt that doesn't serve you. Include statements like:

- "I give myself permission to prioritize my mental health"
- "I give myself permission to say no without justification"
- "I give myself permission to be imperfect and still worthy of love"
- "I give myself permission to outgrow family expectations"
- "I give myself permission to create boundaries that protect my well-being"

Moving Forward: From Guilt to Authentic Choice

Recent research has explored how effective guilt really is in changing behaviors, and though evidence suggests the emotion does have positive prosocial results, it also indicates the potential for negative effects as well. Chronic or toxic guilt can lead to anxiety, depression, and even a compromised immune system. Those after-effects are the opposite of what guilt should produce. In its truest form, guilt should promote personal responsibility—and empathy—rather than an unstable mental state.

The goal isn't to eliminate all guilt—healthy guilt serves an important function in helping us recognize when we've genuinely hurt someone or acted against our values. The goal is to distinguish between healthy guilt that promotes growth and toxic guilt that perpetuates control.

As you begin to recognize and release toxic guilt, you may experience:

- Initial increase in anxiety: As you stop complying automatically, your nervous system may react with fear
- Pushback from family members: They may escalate their guilt tactics when they realize their usual methods aren't working
- Grief: You may mourn the loss of the family dynamics you hoped could be different
- Liberation: Gradually, you'll experience the freedom that comes with making choices based on your values rather than others' expectations

Remember that breaking free from inherited guilt and obligation patterns is not a betrayal of love—it's an act of self-love that creates space for healthier, more authentic relationships. You cannot love others genuinely when you're operating from a place of guilt and obligation. True love, including love for family, can only flourish when it's freely given rather than extracted through manipulation.

The invisible contracts you inherited were never actually binding because you never truly consented to them. You have the power to renegotiate the terms of your relationships or, if necessary, to walk away from contracts that require you to sacrifice your well-being for others' comfort.

Your journey toward emotional freedom begins with this simple truth: you are not responsible for managing other people's emotions, maintaining their comfort, or sacrificing your authenticity to preserve dysfunctional family dynamics. You are responsible for your own healing, your own choices, and your own path toward becoming the person you were meant to be before guilt convinced you otherwise.

Chapter 3: Boundaries Without Apology

Boundaries are not walls to keep people out, but rather gates that allow you to control who enters your space and how they treat you once they're there.

The word "boundaries" has become something of a buzzword in recent years, but for those dealing with toxic family dynamics, boundaries aren't trendy self-help concepts—they're essential survival tools. Setting boundaries is an effective way you maintain a healthy balance in your life and relationships. Knowing how to set boundaries is something we should all learn to do.

Yet for many people raised in toxic family systems, the very concept of boundaries feels foreign, selfish, or even dangerous. You may have been taught that good family members don't have limits, that love means always being available, or that setting boundaries is a form of rejection or abandonment. These messages run deep, but they're fundamentally untrue.

Why Boundaries Are Necessary

Boundaries are standards you're setting to describe how you want to be treated—and you can respect that promise by taking action any time there's a violation and your well-being is at risk. They're not about controlling others; they're about controlling your own life experience and protecting your emotional, physical, and mental well-being.

In toxic family systems, boundaries are often nonexistent or constantly violated. Zero boundaries between family members – being close is one thing, but healthy relationships also have a sense of autonomy. Examples of lack of boundaries: having no personal space, family members walking into your room and going through your personal things, reading diaries, listening in to phone calls.

Without boundaries, you become responsible for managing everyone else's emotions while neglecting your own needs. You lose yourself in the process of trying to keep the peace, avoid conflict, or earn love and approval. Boundaries restore your power and remind you that you have the right to take up space, have preferences, and protect yourself from harm.

The Physical Impact of Boundary Violations

When your boundaries are consistently crossed, your body keeps score. Physical symptoms after interactions should serve as a signal that the dynamic is not serving you: feeling drained, back and neck pain, jaw-clenching, digestive troubles, or a tightness in your stomach. These aren't signs of weakness—they're your body's alarm system telling you that something is wrong.

The Emotional Toll

Living without boundaries in toxic family relationships can lead to:

- Chronic anxiety and hypervigilance
- Depression and feelings of helplessness
- Loss of identity and self-worth
- Difficulty trusting your own judgment
- Resentment that builds over time
- Physical symptoms of stress and tension

Understanding What Boundaries Really Are

The thing to understand about setting clear boundaries with family — or anyone else in your life, for that matter — is that your boundaries are just that…yours. Personal boundaries are the limits you set to establish what's acceptable and within your comfort zone.

Boundaries are not:

- Demands that others change their behavior
- Ultimatums designed to control or manipulate
- Punishments for past wrongs
- Walls that shut everyone out permanently
- Reasons to feel guilty or ashamed

Boundaries are:

- Personal standards for how you want to be treated
- Limits on what you will and won't accept
- Guidelines for your own behavior and responses
- Tools for self-protection and self-care
- Ways to create healthier relationship dynamics
- Necessary for a life of balance, peace, and happiness

Think of boundaries as property lines around your emotional and physical space. Just as you wouldn't allow strangers to walk into your home uninvited, you don't have to allow others unlimited access to your time, energy, emotions, or personal life.

Types of Family Boundaries

Emotional Boundaries

These protect your feelings and emotional well-being:

- "I won't discuss my personal relationships with you"
- "When you raise your voice, I will leave the conversation"
- "I don't want to hear negative comments about my life choices"
- "I need you to stop giving me unsolicited advice about my parenting"

Physical Boundaries

These protect your body and personal space:

- "I'm not comfortable with unexpected hugs or kisses"
- "Please don't come to my home without calling first"
- "I need my own bedroom when I visit"
- "Don't go through my personal belongings"

Time Boundaries

These protect your schedule and availability:

- "I can only visit for two hours on Sunday afternoon"
- "I won't be available for phone calls after 9 PM"
- "I need advance notice if you want me to attend family events"
- "I can't be the primary caregiver anymore"

Financial Boundaries

These protect your resources and financial autonomy:

- "I won't lend money anymore"
- "I'm not comfortable discussing my salary or savings"
- "I won't pay for family events I didn't agree to attend"
- "I need to be consulted before you make financial decisions that affect me"

Communication Boundaries

These protect how and when you communicate:

- "I won't respond to angry text messages"
- "Please don't call me at work unless it's an emergency"

- "I don't want to be included in any gossip"
- "I need you to speak to me directly rather than through other family members"

Topic Boundaries

These protect you from harmful or triggering conversations:

- "I won't discuss my mental health with you"
- "My romantic relationships are off-limits for criticism"
- "I don't want to hear about drama, period"
- "Politics is not a topic I'm willing to debate with you"

How to Set Boundaries: A Step-by-Step Guide

Step 1: Get Clear on Your Needs and Limits

Before you can communicate boundaries to others, you need to understand them yourself. Learning how to set boundaries starts with a self-evaluation and a clear understanding of your values and beliefs. Setting healthy boundaries for dealing with toxic situations can mean identifying, avoiding, and eliminating triggers such as behavior-altering substances, inappropriate topics of conversation, and points of contention that lead to conflict.

Reflection Questions:

- What situations with family members make you feel anxious, angry, or drained?
- When do you feel like your privacy is being invaded?
- What topics of conversation consistently lead to conflict or upset you?
- What expectations do family members have of you that feel unreasonable?
- What have you tolerated in the past that you won't tolerate anymore?

Step 2: Start Small and Be Specific

Don't try to set every boundary at once. Choose one or two specific areas to focus on initially. Be concrete rather than vague. Remember: setting boundaries is something that evolves over time and can be updated as situations arise.

Instead of: "I need more respect"

Try: "I need you to stop commenting on my appearance when I visit"

Instead of: "You're too demanding"

Try: "I can visit once a month, but I can't commit to weekly visits right now"

Step 3: Use "I" Statements

Frame boundaries from your perspective rather than as accusations or demands about the other person's behavior.

Examples:

- "I feel overwhelmed when you call me multiple times a day. I need to limit our phone conversations to once a week."
- "I'm not comfortable discussing my finances. I won't be answering questions about my income or spending."
- "I need to leave when conversations become heated. If voices are raised, I'll step away until we can talk calmly."

Step 4: Be Clear About Consequences

Setting boundaries may seem uncomfortable and challenging at first, but remember, a clear boundary can help you feel safe and protected even if others don't always like it or agree with you. For example, you may decide that you need time to yourself each day, and you have the right to take that time even if others think differently.

A boundary without a consequence is just a request. You need to be prepared to follow through on what you'll do if the boundary is crossed.

Examples:

- "If you continue to criticize my partner, I will end the conversation and leave"
- "If you show up at my house uninvited, I won't answer the door"
- "If you bring up topics I've asked you not to discuss, I will change the subject or leave"
- "If you send me angry text messages, I won't respond until you can communicate respectfully"

Step 5: Practice Your Delivery

Practice saying no or demanding that your boundaries are respected ahead of time. Rehearse your boundary statements until they feel natural. Consider practicing with a trusted friend or therapist who can help you refine your approach.

Tips for Delivery:

- Speak calmly and clearly
- Maintain steady eye contact
- Keep your voice neutral, not defensive or aggressive
- Don't over-explain or justify your boundaries
- Be prepared for pushback, but don't let it derail you

Communicating Boundaries Effectively

The JADE Trap: Don't Justify, Argue, Defend, or Explain

One of the biggest mistakes people make when setting boundaries is falling into the JADE trap. When family members push back against your boundaries (and they likely will), resist the urge to:

Justify: "I'm setting this boundary because..."

Argue: "You're wrong, and here's why..."

Defend: "I have every right to..."

Explain: "Let me help you understand..."

Instead, simply restate your boundary: "I understand you're upset, but this boundary is important for my well-being, and I'm going to maintain it."

Use Values-Based Language

If she persists no matter how many times you say no, try offering a values-based reason for declining: "I love that food, and I enjoyed the small amount I had. I'm focusing on my health right now, and what makes me feel really good is having just a little bit." That way, you're explaining what your values are, rather than simply saying, "I don't want it." Then ask your mom about her values: "I hear you repeatedly asking me to eat this. What is it that my eating it would communicate to you?"

Connecting your boundaries to your values can help family members understand that this isn't about rejecting them personally—it's about living in alignment with what matters to you.

Be Consistent

You cannot expect toxic family members to respect your boundaries after one serious conversation. You should stand firm and maintain your personal boundaries; do not waver. Consistency is crucial. If you enforce a boundary sometimes but not others, you're teaching people that your boundaries are negotiable.

Stay Calm and Compassionate

Setting boundaries doesn't necessarily mean you have to be callous. In fact, when you build your boundaries with those difficult family members, it can actually be more effective to do it with kindness. Anger or defensiveness will only rile them up and cause them to lash out at you.

You can be firm and kind at the same time. Remember, boundaries aren't about punishment—they're about protection.

Responding to Boundary Violations and Pushback

When you start setting boundaries with toxic family members, expect pushback. This is normal and often indicates that your boundaries are necessary. People engaging in toxic behavior are often resistant to change. If a difficult family member consistently oversteps your boundaries, would clearer communication help, or are they likely to continue their behavior regardless of what you say?

Common Forms of Pushback

Guilt-Tripping:

"After everything I've done for you, this is how you repay me?"

Response: "I understand you're hurt. This boundary isn't about our history—it's about creating a healthier relationship moving forward."

Minimizing:

"You're being too sensitive. It's not that big a deal."

Response: "This is important to me, and I need you to respect it."

Anger and Tantrums:

Yelling, name-calling, or explosive reactions

Response: "I can see you're upset. I'm going to take a break until we can talk calmly."

Playing the Victim:

"You're hurting the whole family. Everyone thinks you've changed."

Response: "I'm sorry you feel that way. This is what I need to do for my well-being."

Testing:

Repeatedly violating the boundary to see if you'll enforce it

Response: Follow through with your stated consequences every single time

Silent Treatment:

Withdrawing affection or communication as punishment

Response: Don't chase them. Use the space to strengthen your resolve.

The Extinction Burst

When you first set boundaries, expect what psychologists call an "extinction burst"—a temporary increase in the problematic behavior as the person tries harder to get you to return to the old patterns. This is actually a sign that your boundaries are working. Stay consistent, and the behavior will eventually decrease.

When to Walk Away

You never have to stay in a situation that feels dangerous or toxic. If your boundaries are not being respected, you can always leave. You can try to talk through things if you feel that's the best route to go, but at a certain point, especially if it's been difficult for any amount of time, you can always simply leave.

You don't need to apologize, and you don't need to explain to anybody else unless you want to. You've set your boundaries, and if they're not being respected, then you can remove yourself from the situation, guilt-free.

The Gray Rock Method: A Boundary Technique for High-Conflict Situations

Sometimes, especially when you're financially dependent on toxic family members or can't avoid contact, the gray rock method can be an effective boundary technique. The Grey Rock method is essentially what the name suggests. It involves being neutral regardless of the conversation and circumstance. Avoid engaging in heated arguments and be as balanced as possible.

The gray rock method involves:

- Giving minimal responses ("okay," "I see," "mm-hmm")
- Avoiding emotional reactions
- Sharing no personal information
- Being polite but boring

- Not taking the bait for arguments or drama

The goal is to become so uninteresting that the toxic person loses interest in targeting you for drama or manipulation.

Maintaining Boundaries Long-Term

Remember Your Why

A big part of setting healthy boundaries is believing that you're in charge of your own life. Once you do the hard part — set the boundaries — you need to remember you have the strength and power to enforce them.

Keep a written reminder of why each boundary is important to you. When you're tempted to give in or when guilt starts creeping in, read this reminder to strengthen your resolve.

Build a Support System

If there are members of your family who do genuinely value you, seek them out and use them to help you set boundaries with the family members who don't seem to value you. If there aren't any members of your family who can help you with this, find people outside the circle of your family. Your friend group is a good place to start. You are bound to have at least one friend who can help you start to build the boundaries that you need.

Surround yourself with people who support your right to have boundaries and who won't try to talk you out of protecting yourself.

Take Care of Yourself

Boundary-setting can be emotionally exhausting, especially in the beginning. Make sure you're practicing good self-care:

- Get enough sleep
- Exercise regularly
- Eat nutritious meals
- Practice stress-reduction techniques
- Consider therapy or counseling
- Engage in activities that bring you joy

Expect Boundaries to Evolve

As much as possible, be fluid: The boundaries you set today might need to change in a month or in a year or two. No matter how they evolve, their core function—protecting your well-being—remains the same.

Boundaries aren't set in stone. As you grow and change, and as relationships evolve, you may need to adjust your boundaries. This is normal and healthy.

Practicing Confidence Through Repetition

The more you practice setting and maintaining boundaries, the more natural it becomes. Tell yourself that nobody can make you feel anything. Nobody can make you do anything. You are in charge. You expect those around you to respect your boundaries.

Start with small, low-stakes boundaries to build your confidence before tackling the bigger, more challenging ones. Each time you successfully maintain a boundary, you're reinforcing your right to protect yourself and proving to yourself that you can do this.

Common Boundary-Setting Phrases to Practice

- "I'm not comfortable with that"
- "That doesn't work for me"
- "I need some time to think about it"
- "I'm not available for that"
- "I'd prefer not to discuss this"
- "This isn't a good time for me"
- "I've made other plans"
- "I need to step away from this conversation"
- "I won't be participating in that"
- "I understand you're disappointed, but my answer is no"

Common Boundary-Setting Mistakes to Avoid

1. Setting Boundaries When You're Angry

While anger can motivate you to finally set boundaries, it's better to have these conversations when you're calm and clear-headed. Anger can make your boundaries sound like attacks, which will likely trigger defensiveness.

2. Setting Too Many Boundaries at Once

This can feel overwhelming. Start with the most important ones and build gradually.

3. Making Boundaries About Changing Others

Remember, boundaries are about controlling your own behavior and responses, not about forcing others to change.

4. Not Following Through on Consequences

If you don't follow through, you're teaching people that your boundaries are empty threats.

5. Negotiating Non-Negotiable Boundaries

Boundaries should be firm and non-negotiable. Don't let manipulation tactics convince you to compromise on things that are truly important to your well-being.

6. Apologizing for Your Boundaries

You don't need to apologize for protecting yourself. Boundaries aren't something to feel guilty about.

When Boundaries Aren't Enough

Sometimes, despite your best efforts to set and maintain boundaries, toxic family members continue to violate them. If repeated efforts go unheeded, and the relationship is unmanageable with the methods mentioned earlier, consider cutting ties. Sometimes, the only way to deal with toxic relationships is to remove yourself from the equation as a form of self-care. Despite what people may say, you need to protect yourself from such abusive relationships.

It's important to recognize when boundaries alone aren't sufficient to protect your well-being. This realization doesn't mean you've failed—it means you're prioritizing your mental health and safety.

Reflection Exercises: Building Your Boundary Foundation

Exercise 1: Boundary Inventory

Take some time to reflect on your current family relationships and identify areas where boundaries might be helpful.

For each family member who causes you stress or discomfort, consider:

- What specific behaviors or actions make you feel uncomfortable, angry, or drained?
- How do you currently respond to these behaviors?
- What would you like to be different about your interactions with this person?
- What boundaries might help protect your well-being in this relationship?
- What are you afraid might happen if you set boundaries with this person?
- How do you think setting boundaries might actually improve the relationship?

Exercise 2: Values Clarification

Understanding your core values will help you set boundaries that align with who you are and what matters most to you.

Complete these sentences:

- I feel most authentic and true to myself when...
- The values that guide my life decisions are...
- I feel violated or disrespected when someone...
- I am willing to tolerate... but I will not tolerate...
- In healthy relationships, I expect...
- The kind of treatment I deserve is...

Exercise 3: Physical and Emotional Body Scan

Your body often knows when boundaries are needed before your mind does.

Think about interactions with difficult family members and notice:

- Where do you feel tension in your body during or after these interactions?
- What emotions come up most frequently?
- How does your energy level change?
- What physical symptoms do you experience?
- How long does it take you to feel "normal" again after these interactions?

These physical and emotional responses are valuable information about where boundaries are needed.

Exercise 4: Boundary Visualization

Imagine you have successfully set and maintained healthy boundaries with your family members.

- How would your relationships feel different?
- What would change about family gatherings or communications?
- How would you feel about yourself?
- What activities or interests might you pursue if you weren't constantly managing family drama?
- How would your other relationships benefit?

Exercise 5: Support System Assessment

Identify the people in your life who:

- Support your right to have boundaries
- Encourage your growth and well-being
- Respect your decisions even when they don't understand them
- Offer practical help when you need it
- Listen without trying to fix or minimize your experiences

If your support system feels limited, brainstorm ways to:

- Strengthen existing supportive relationships
- Meet new people who share your values
- Find professional support (therapists, support groups)
- Connect with online communities of people with similar experiences

Boundary-Setting Worksheet

Use this worksheet to plan and practice setting specific boundaries with family members.

Boundary Planning Template

Family Member: _____

Specific Behavior/Situation That Needs a Boundary: _____

How This Behavior/Situation Affects Me: _____

The Boundary I Want to Set: _____

How I Will Communicate This Boundary: (Practice writing out exactly what you'll say) _____

Potential Pushback I Might Receive: _____

How I Will Respond to Pushback: _____

The Consequence I Will Implement if This Boundary is Violated: _____

Support I Need to Maintain This Boundary: _____

When and Where I Will Communicate This Boundary: _____

Boundary Success Tracker

Use this tracker to monitor your progress and celebrate your successes.

Date: _____

Boundary Set: _____

How It Went: _____

Challenges Encountered: _____

What I Learned: _____

What I'll Do Differently Next Time: _____

How I Feel About My Progress: _____

Emergency Boundary Responses

For times when you need to set an immediate boundary in the moment:

When someone is:

- Yelling or being verbally aggressive: _____
- Violating your physical space: _____
- Demanding your time/energy: _____
- Giving unwanted advice: _____
- Gossiping or creating drama: _____
- Making inappropriate comments: _____

Quick Boundary Phrases I Can Use:

Remember: You have the right to protect yourself, your time, your energy, and your well-being. Boundaries aren't selfish; they're essential. Every small step you take toward honoring your own needs is an act of self-respect and courage.

Standing up for yourself is not selfish but a display of strength and self-love. Though people say family is for life, enduring toxicity is a choice.

Chapter 4: The Backlash Is Real

"The only way to make sense out of change is to plunge into it, move with it, and join the dance." — Alan Watts

When you begin to pull away from toxic family dynamics and assert your boundaries, you enter what many therapists call "the eye of the storm." When you set boundaries, it usually upsets the people who are taking advantage of you. Expect protests, guilt trips, or icy silences. This chapter prepares you for what's coming and gives you the tools to weather the inevitable backlash with your sanity and resolve intact.

The Predictable Storm

The backlash isn't a sign that you're doing something wrong—it's confirmation that you're doing something right. People engaging in toxic behavior are often resistant to change. If a difficult family member consistently oversteps your boundaries, would clearer communication help, or are they likely to continue their behavior regardless of what you say?

Toxic family members react strongly to boundaries for several reasons:

Loss of Control: Your boundaries threaten their ability to manipulate and control you. When you stop being predictable and compliant, they lose a significant source of power.

Disruption of the System: Family systems resist change. When you shift your role, it forces everyone else to adjust, creating discomfort throughout the entire family structure.

Narcissistic Injury: For family members with narcissistic traits, your boundaries feel like personal attacks on their identity and worth.

Fear of Abandonment: Paradoxically, some toxic behaviors stem from deep fears of being left alone. Your boundaries may trigger these primal fears.

Loss of Benefits: If family members have been getting something from your compliance—emotional regulation, financial support, or ego stroking—they'll fight to maintain those benefits.

The Escalation Playbook: What to Expect

When you start setting boundaries with family, pushback is common. Family members might not understand or may feel hurt by the changes. Having a few prepared responses can help you be clear, compassionate, and firm, and handle these situations with confidence and empathy.

Here's what the backlash typically looks like:

Phase 1: Testing and Probing (The First Few Weeks)

Boundary Testing: They'll deliberately violate your boundaries to see if you're serious. Expect "accidental" calls during your stated no-contact hours or surprise visits after you've asked for space.

Selective Hearing: They'll claim they "didn't understand" or "forgot" your clearly stated boundaries. This is rarely genuine confusion.

Minimization: "You're being too sensitive." "It's not that serious." "You're overreacting." They'll try to make your boundaries seem unreasonable.

Historical Revisionism: Suddenly, they might claim past incidents never happened or weren't "that bad." They're trying to undermine your justification for boundaries.

Phase 2: Emotional Manipulation (Weeks 2-6)

The Guilt Trip Highway: Expect masterful guilt trips. "I guess I'm just a terrible mother." "After everything I've done for you." "You're breaking up the family."

Playing the Victim: They'll position themselves as the wronged party. You become the unreasonable, ungrateful, selfish family member who's hurting everyone.

Love Bombing: Sudden excessive affection, gifts, or promises to change. This is designed to pull you back into the old pattern before you fully establish your boundaries.

Health Scares: Mysterious illnesses or exaggerated health problems that require your immediate attention and care.

Holiday and Special Event Manipulation: They'll use birthdays, holidays, and family celebrations to pressure you into abandoning your boundaries "just this once."

Phase 3: Escalation and Consequences (Months 2-6)

Flying Monkeys Deployed: Other family members, friends, or even family acquaintances may suddenly contact you to "talk sense into you" or share how "hurt" the toxic family member is.

Social Media Warfare: Passive-aggressive posts about ungrateful children, broken families, or how some people "abandon" their loved ones. They might share old photos with captions about "better times."

Smear Campaigns: They'll tell anyone who will listen to their version of events, painting you as unstable, ungrateful, or mentally ill.

Financial Threats: If they have any financial leverage over you, they may threaten to cut off support, change wills, or demand repayment of past "gifts."

Legal Threats: In extreme cases, they might threaten legal action, grandparents' rights claims, or involve authorities with false reports.

Escalated Contact Attempts: When their usual methods fail, they might show up at your workplace, home, or contact your friends and colleagues.

Losing Mutual Connections

One of the most painful aspects of setting boundaries with toxic family members is the collateral damage to other relationships. When setting boundaries, individuals may encounter opposition, often manifesting as emotional manipulation or attempts to induce guilt. Mental health professionals emphasize the importance of maintaining consistent boundaries, even in the face of resistance, to protect one's well-being and promote healthier family dynamics.

The Family Divide

Not everyone will understand or support your decision to set boundaries.

Some family members will:

Take Sides: They may feel forced to choose between maintaining their relationship with you or the toxic family member.

Minimize Your Experience: "That's just how they are." "They mean well." "Can't you just get along?"

Become Flying Monkeys: They'll pressure you to "keep the peace" or "be the bigger person" by abandoning your boundaries.

Distance Themselves: Some family members may pull away from you to avoid being caught in the middle or because they're uncomfortable with conflict.

Friends and Extended Network

Your social circle might also be affected:

- Longtime family friends may only know one side of the story
- Neighbors and community members might receive a distorted version of events
- Social invitations may become awkward or stop altogether
- Mutual friends may feel uncomfortable or pressured to choose sides

Protecting Yourself During the Divide

Remember these crucial points:

- You cannot control other people's reactions to your boundaries
- People who pressure you to accept toxic treatment aren't truly supportive of your well-being
- Quality relationships are more valuable than quantity
- True friends and healthy family members will respect your boundaries, even if they don't fully understand them

Emotional Preparation: Building Your Fortress

To manage backlash effectively, individuals can employ various coping strategies, including prioritizing sleep hygiene and limiting alcohol consumption. These practices can help maintain emotional stability and clarity of reason when faced with challenging family interactions. Additionally, seeking support through therapy or engaging with mental health podcasts can provide valuable insights and techniques for navigating complex family relationships.

Mental Preparation Strategies

Expect the Worst, Hope for the Best: Mentally prepare for the maximum level of backlash. This isn't pessimism—it's strategic planning. When you're prepared for the storm, you're less likely to be knocked off course by it.

Develop Your Mantra: Create a personal statement that reinforces your decision.

Examples:

- "I am not responsible for managing other people's emotions."
- "My well-being matters, and I deserve healthy relationships."
- "Setting boundaries is an act of self-love, not selfishness."
- "I cannot change them, but I can change how I respond."

Create an Evidence File: Write down specific incidents that led to your decision to set boundaries. When doubt creeps in (and it will), refer back to these documented experiences.

Prepare Standard Responses: Have ready responses for common manipulation tactics:

- "I understand you're upset, but my boundary remains the same."
- "This is what works best for me right now."
- "I'm not willing to discuss this further."
- "I can see this conversation isn't productive. I'm going to end it now."
- "This is what I need to do to protect myself right now."

Physical and Emotional Self-Care

Sleep Hygiene: Prioritize 7-9 hours of quality sleep. Stress and emotional manipulation are harder to handle when you're exhausted.

Nutrition: Maintain regular, nutritious meals. Stress can affect appetite, but your body needs fuel to handle emotional challenges.

Exercise: Regular physical activity helps process stress hormones and maintain emotional equilibrium.

Mindfulness and Meditation: Even 10 minutes daily of mindfulness practice can significantly improve your ability to stay centered during difficult interactions.

Limit Substances: Avoid using alcohol or other substances to cope with the stress of boundary-setting. These can cloud your judgment and weaken your resolve.

Building Your Support Network

Identify Your Core Supporters: Make a list of people who truly support your well-being, regardless of family pressure.

Professional Support: Consider working with a therapist who understands toxic family dynamics and can provide objective guidance.

Support Groups: Online and in-person support groups for people with toxic families can provide validation and practical advice.

Trusted Friends: Cultivate relationships with friends who respect boundaries and support your right to protect yourself.

Protecting Yourself: Practical Strategies

Digital Protection

Social Media Boundaries:

- Consider blocking or unfriending toxic family members temporarily or permanently
- Consider blocking other people who have any contact with family members
- Adjust privacy settings so they can't see your posts or activities
- Be cautious about what you share publicly during this period
- Ask trusted friends not to share information about you with family members

Communication Management:

- Use blocking features on phone and email when necessary
- Create separate email addresses for essential communication
- Consider using a Google Voice number for family contact if a complete no-contact isn't feasible
- Save voicemails and text messages as evidence if harassment escalates

Physical Safety

Home Security:

- Consider changing locks if family members have keys
- Install security cameras if you're concerned about unexpected visits
- Inform trusted neighbors about your situation
- Have a safety plan if you feel physically threatened

Workplace Boundaries:

- Inform your supervisor or HR department if family members might contact your workplace
- Have a security escort unexpected family visitors from the premises
- Keep personal information private from colleagues

Legal Considerations

Document Everything:

- Keep records of all communications, including dates, times, and content
- Save voicemails, text messages, emails, and social media posts
- Document any instances of harassment, threats, or violations of your boundaries
- Take screenshots of social media posts that might be deleted later

Know Your Rights:

- Research restraining order options in your jurisdiction
- Understand workplace harassment policies
- Know your rights regarding grandparents' rights or other family legal threats
- Consult with an attorney if threats escalate

Riding Out the Storm: Long-Term Strategies

Maintaining Perspective

Remember this is Temporary: The intensity of the backlash typically decreases over time. Most toxic family members eventually realize their tactics aren't working and either adjust their behavior or reduce contact.

Focus on Your Progress: Keep a journal of positive changes in your life since setting boundaries. This helps counteract gaslighting and doubt.

Celebrate Small Victories: Acknowledge every successful boundary enforcement, no matter how small it seems.

Staying Strong Under Pressure

The Broken Record Technique: Repeat your boundary calmly and consistently without elaborating or defending. "That doesn't work for me." "My decision remains the same." "I'm not available for that."

Gray Rock During Forced Contact: If you must interact with the toxic family member, be as uninteresting as possible. Give short, factual answers without emotional content.

Planned Responses: Have exit strategies for every situation. Know how you'll leave family gatherings, end phone calls, or disengage from conflicts.

Managing Guilt and Doubt

Normalize Your Feelings: Feeling guilty about setting boundaries is normal, especially in toxic family systems where guilt has been used as a control mechanism your entire life.

Question the Guilt: Ask yourself:

- Would I feel guilty about protecting myself from a stranger who treated me this way?
- Is this guilt mine, or has it been programmed into me?
- What would I tell a friend in my situation?

Reframe Your Perspective:

You're not abandoning your family—you're refusing to participate in dysfunction. You're not being cruel—you're being honest about what you need to maintain your well-being.

Building Your Emotional Toolkit

Immediate Response Tools

The STOP Technique:

- **S**top what you're doing
- **T**ake a breath
- **O**bserve your emotions and physical sensations
- **P**roceed with intention rather than reaction

The 5-4-3-2-1 Grounding Technique:

- **5** things you can see
- **4** things you can touch
- **3** things you can hear
- **2** things you can smell

- **1** thing you can taste

This helps you stay present and grounded during difficult interactions.

Physical Grounding:

- Press your feet firmly into the ground
- Hold a cold object or splash cold water on your face
- Do jumping jacks or push-ups to discharge stress energy
- Use progressive muscle relaxation
- Readjust your body if you're sitting down

Long-term Emotional Regulation

Daily Check-ins: Spend 5-10 minutes each day assessing your emotional state and stress levels.

Stress Journal: Track what triggers your stress and what helps you cope. Look for patterns and adjust your strategies accordingly.

Professional Processing: Regular therapy sessions to process the ongoing stress and maintain perspective.

Creative Outlets: Art, writing, music, or other creative expressions can help process complex emotions.

Red Flags: When Professional Help is Needed

Sometimes the backlash escalates beyond normal family conflict. Seek professional help immediately if you experience:

Immediate Safety Concerns

- Physical threats or violence
- Stalking behavior
- Threats of self-harm by family members as manipulation
- Substance abuse escalation in response to your boundaries
- Involvement of your children in manipulation or threats

Legal Issues

- False police reports or CPS calls
- Identity theft or financial sabotage

- Threats of legal action
- Harassment at work or school
- Violation of restraining orders

Mental Health Crisis

- Thoughts of self-harm
- Severe anxiety or panic attacks
- Depression that interferes with daily functioning
- Substance abuse as a coping mechanism
- Complete social isolation

Supporting Others Through Your Journey

If You Have Children

Age-Appropriate Honesty: Explain the situation in terms children can understand without burdening them with adult problems.

Maintain Stability: Keep routines and stability in your children's lives despite family upheaval.

Professional Support: Consider family therapy or counseling for children who are affected by the family conflict.

Protect from Manipulation: Be vigilant about toxic family members trying to use your children against you or involving them in adult conflicts.

If You Have a Partner

United Front: Ensure you and your partner are aligned on boundaries and responses to family backlash.

Support Their Feelings: Your partner may have their own complex feelings about the situation, especially if they were close to your family.

Protect the Relationship: Don't let family toxicity poison your primary relationship. Consider couples therapy if needed.

Boundaries for Partners: Clarify what role, if any, your partner should play in enforcing boundaries with your family.

Reflection: Identifying Red Flags and Building Your Toolkit

Reflection Exercise: Your Personal Red Flag List

Take time to identify and write down the specific behaviors that signal escalating toxicity in your family. This awareness helps you respond rather than react.

Communication Red Flags:

- What phrases or tone of voice immediately put you on edge?
- How do you know when a conversation is turning manipulative?
- What topics always lead to conflict or manipulation?

Behavioral Red Flags:

- What behaviors make you feel unsafe or violated?
- How do you recognize when someone is testing your boundaries?
- What actions signal that someone is escalating their tactics?

Emotional Red Flags:

- How does your body feel when you're being manipulated?
- What emotions typically come up during toxic interactions?
- When do you notice yourself starting to doubt your boundaries?

Building Your Personal Emergency Kit

Create a collection of tools and resources you can access quickly during difficult moments:

Physical Comfort Items:

- A weighted blanket for anxiety
- Essential oils or calming scents
- Comfortable clothes for stress days
- A journal for processing emotions
- Bath bombs or scented Epsom salts for a warm, relaxing bath

Digital Resources:

- Playlist of calming or empowering music
- Photos that remind you of your progress and strength
- Contact list of supportive friends and professionals

- Apps for meditation, breathing, or anxiety management

Reference Materials:

- This book (especially chapters that speak to you)
- Quotes or affirmations that ground you
- Your list of reasons for setting boundaries
- Evidence of positive changes since boundary-setting

Support Network:

- Therapist's contact information
- Crisis hotline numbers
- Trusted friends who understand your situation
- Support group information

Weekly Boundary Check-In

Schedule a weekly time to assess how your boundaries are holding up.

Questions to Ask Yourself:

- Which boundaries were tested this week?
- How did I respond?
- What worked well?
- What would I do differently?
- What support do I need for the coming week?
- How is my overall well-being?

Action Items: Adjust boundaries if needed

- Plan responses to anticipated challenges
- Schedule self-care activities
- Reach out for support if necessary

Remember: This Too Shall Pass

The backlash period is intense but usually temporary. Discomfort isn't danger—stay the course. Most toxic family members eventually realize their manipulation tactics aren't working and either modify their behavior or reduce contact. Some may even respect your boundaries once they understand you're serious about maintaining them.

What feels overwhelming and never-ending right now is actually a necessary phase of establishing your new normal. Every boundary you maintain, every manipulation tactic you resist, and every day you prioritize your well-being over family expectations is moving you toward a healthier, more authentic life.

The storm is real, but so is your strength. You've survived their toxicity for years—you can certainly survive their reaction to your refusal to accept it any longer. I believe that you can do hard things. The fact that you have survived that, and that you're even considering moving differently in that family dynamic, is a testament to your resilience and ability to do hard things. And I'm sorry you've had to be so strong.

Your future self—the one living freely, authentically, and without the constant stress of toxic family dynamics—is cheering you on from the other side of this storm. Keep going. You've got this.

Chapter 5: Forgiveness Isn't About Them

"Forgiveness is not a gift you give to someone who hurt you. It's a gift you give to yourself." - Unknown

When we talk about forgiveness in the context of toxic family relationships, most people immediately tense up. From an early age, we're shaped to believe there's only one "right" way to relate to our parents. You're supposed to have a certain relationship with your siblings. Forgiveness is often weaponized as another tool to keep us trapped in harmful dynamics.

But what if everything you've been taught about forgiveness is wrong?

What if forgiveness isn't about absolving your family members of their harmful behavior, restoring relationships, or pretending the past didn't happen? What if, instead, forgiveness is entirely about freeing yourself from the prison of resentment and pain that keeps you bound to the very people who hurt you?

This chapter will challenge everything you think you know about forgiveness and help you discover a path to healing that serves you—not your toxic family members.

The Forgiveness Trap We've Been Taught

From childhood, most of us are taught a version of forgiveness that serves everyone except the person doing the forgiving. We're told that "good people" forgive, that holding onto anger makes us bitter, and that we must forgive family members because "they're family." Forgiving a family member does not mean you have to forget, yet the pressure to not only forgive but also reconcile remains immense.

This traditional understanding of forgiveness often includes several toxic elements:

Forgiveness as Obligation: You're told you "must" forgive because it's the "right" thing to do, regardless of whether the person has acknowledged their wrongdoing or changed their behavior.

Forgiveness as Reconciliation: The assumption that forgiving someone means you have to restore the relationship and allow them back into your life.

Forgiveness as Amnesia: The expectation that true forgiveness means forgetting what happened and never bringing it up again.

Forgiveness as Urgency: The pressure to forgive quickly, before you've fully processed the harm or grief you've experienced.

Forgiveness as Absolution: The belief that your forgiveness somehow erases the other person's responsibility for their actions.

This distorted version of forgiveness often leaves victims feeling guilty for their natural reactions to abuse and trauma. It places the burden of healing the relationship on the person who was harmed rather than on the person who caused the harm. And perhaps most damaging of all, it suggests that your pain is less important than maintaining family harmony.

Redefining Forgiveness: What It Really Is

True forgiveness is radically different from what most of us have been taught. It appears that forgiveness really is a gift you give yourself. Let's explore what forgiveness actually means when it's understood correctly.

Forgiveness is an internal process. It happens within you, for you, and doesn't require anything from the person who hurt you. They don't need to know about it, acknowledge it, or participate in it in any way.

Forgiveness is about releasing resentment, not excusing behavior. When you forgive, you're not saying what happened was okay. You're saying you're no longer willing to carry the poison of resentment in your body and mind.

Forgiveness is separate from reconciliation. You can forgive someone and still choose to have no contact with them. You can forgive someone and still maintain strict boundaries. Forgiveness doesn't obligate you to restore a relationship.

Forgiveness is a process, not an event. It's not something you do once and it's finished. It may take years, and that's completely normal. Some days you may feel forgiving, others you may not, and both are okay.

Forgiveness includes anger. Being angry about injustice and harm is healthy and appropriate. Forgiveness doesn't mean you can't be angry about what happened to you.

Forgiveness doesn't require forgetting. Forgiveness is not forgetting. According to Markman and colleagues, when people say "forgive and forget," they usually mean putting the wrongdoing in the past and not letting it consume their thinking and feelings. Remembering what happened is actually protective and wise.

Forgiveness is optional. Despite what you may have been told, you are not required to forgive anyone. If forgiveness doesn't serve your healing journey, you have every right to choose a different path.

The Science and Benefits of True Forgiveness

When forgiveness is understood and practiced correctly, the benefits are profound. Scientifically validated benefits of forgiving include the reduction of chronic pain, cardiovascular problems, and violent behavior; increased hope; and decreased levels of depression and anxiety.

Research shows that people who practice healthy forgiveness:

- Have lower blood pressure and heart rates
- Experience less chronic pain
- Report better sleep quality
- Have stronger immune systems
- Show decreased levels of depression and anxiety
- Experience greater emotional stability
- Report higher life satisfaction

But here's the crucial point: these benefits come from the internal process of releasing resentment, not from restoring relationships with those who harmed you. You can still move ahead and forgive. It may be hard, but if you don't, you and the relationship will suffer added damage. You put yourself at risk for psychological and physical problems such as depression, ulcers, high blood pressure, and rage. That's no way to live.

When Forgiveness Isn't the Answer

It's important to acknowledge that forgiveness isn't always the right path for everyone. Some situations and some people may require different approaches to healing:

When safety is at risk: If forgiving someone makes you more vulnerable to ongoing abuse or manipulation, it may not be appropriate.

When it's premature: If you're still in the early stages of recognizing abuse or just beginning to feel anger about your treatment, pushing yourself to forgive may interfere with your natural healing process.

When it's being demanded: If others are pressuring you to forgive, especially the person who harmed you, this is likely manipulation rather than a genuine opportunity for healing.

When it serves the abuser: If your forgiveness primarily benefits the person who hurt you by allowing them to avoid consequences or continue harmful behavior, it may not be serving your best interests.

Instead of working on "forgiving", use the energy to work on "acceptance" and understand that their toxic behavior has nothing to do with you and everything to do with them. Sometimes acceptance is more healing than traditional forgiveness.

Alternative Paths to Healing

If forgiveness doesn't feel right for you, or if it's not serving your healing journey, there are other paths to freedom:

Radical Acceptance: Accepting the reality of what happened without needing to feel differently about it. This involves acknowledging the truth of your experience without trying to change your emotional response.

Focusing on Your Own Growth: Focus on you. It's not being selfish; it is a necessity for your own well-being. You focus on you. Sometimes the most healing thing you can do is redirect the energy you've been spending on forgiveness toward building a better life for yourself.

Seeking Justice: Sometimes healing requires taking action—whether that's legal action, breaking family silence, or simply telling your truth to people who matter to you.

Creating Meaning: Finding ways to use your experience to help others or create positive change in the world can be profoundly healing, even without formal forgiveness.

Grieving: Sometimes we need to grieve the family we never had, the childhood we didn't get, or the relationships that could never be before we can consider forgiveness.

The Forgiveness Letter: A Tool for Healing

One powerful tool for exploring forgiveness is writing a forgiveness letter. This letter is for you and you alone. You will never send it to the person who hurt you. Its purpose is to help you process your emotions and gain clarity about your own healing journey.

Here's how to approach this exercise:

Set Up Your Space: Choose a quiet, private place where you won't be interrupted. Have tissues available, as this process can be emotional.

Write Without Censoring: Don't worry about grammar, spelling, or being "nice." This is your opportunity to express everything you've been holding inside.

Include Everything: Write about the specific incidents that hurt you, how they affected your life, what you wish had been different, and how you feel now.

Express All Your Emotions: Include your anger, sadness, disappointment, fear, and any other emotions you've experienced. Don't judge yourself for having these feelings.

Take Your Time: This doesn't have to be completed in one sitting. You can return to it over days, weeks, or months as new insights emerge.

Decide What to Do with It: After writing, you might choose to keep the letter, burn it in a ceremonial way, bury it, or tear it up. The act of writing is often more important than what you do with the physical letter afterward.

A Different Kind of Forgiveness Letter

Some people discover deep healing in writing a forgiveness letter to themselves—sometimes alongside a letter to the person who hurt them, and sometimes in place of it. This letter acknowledges your own suffering and offers you the compassion you may never have received from others.

A self-forgiveness letter might include:

- Acknowledgment of what you endured
- Recognition of your strength in surviving
- Compassion for the ways you coped, even if they weren't perfect
- Permission to heal at your own pace

- Commitment to treating yourself with kindness moving forward

The Myth of Closure

Our culture often suggests that forgiveness provides "closure"—a final resolution that allows us to move on completely. This is another myth that can be harmful to survivors of family trauma.

Healing isn't linear, and it rarely provides the neat closure that movies and self-help books promise. Instead, healing is an ongoing process of:

- Growing stronger and more resilient
- Developing better boundaries and self-protection skills
- Building healthier relationships
- Creating meaning from your experiences
- Learning to trust yourself and your perceptions
- Finding peace with the complexity of your emotions

You don't need closure to heal. You need permission to be exactly where you are in your healing journey without judgment or pressure to be somewhere else.

Forgiveness and Contact Decisions

One of the most confusing aspects of forgiveness is how it relates to your decisions about contact with toxic family members. People often assume that if you've "truly" forgiven someone, you should be willing to have a relationship with them. This is false.

Forgiveness and boundaries are separate decisions.

You can forgive and go no contact: Releasing resentment doesn't mean exposing yourself to ongoing harm.

You can forgive and maintain limited contact: You might forgive someone but still choose to interact with them only in specific, controlled circumstances.

You can have contact without forgiveness: Sometimes practical considerations require interaction with family members you haven't forgiven, and that's okay too.

Your contact decisions can change: You might forgive someone and later realize that contact still isn't healthy for you, or you might maintain no contact for years and then feel ready to try limited interaction.

The key is making decisions based on what serves your well-being, not on what others think you should do.

When They Want Your Forgiveness

Toxic family members often demand forgiveness, especially once you've started setting boundaries or distancing yourself. They may:

- Claim they've changed (without evidence)
- Minimize their behavior ("It wasn't that bad")
- Blame you for being "unforgiving" or "holding grudges"
- Use other family members to pressure you to forgive
- Make their health or well-being contingent on your forgiveness

Remember: your forgiveness is not owed to anyone. It's not something they can demand, earn through manipulation, or claim as their right. Your forgiveness is yours to give or withhold as it serves your healing.

If someone is pressuring you to forgive them, consider whether this pressure itself is a continuation of the toxic behavior you're trying to heal from.

Forgiveness in Different Life Stages

Your relationship with forgiveness may change as you move through different stages of healing and life.

Early Healing: You may need to focus on recognizing abuse, feeling your anger, and establishing safety. Forgiveness may feel impossible or inappropriate during this stage.

Middle Healing: As you become stronger and more stable, you may start to consider forgiveness as a tool for your own liberation, separate from the needs or demands of your family.

Later Healing: You might find that forgiveness happens naturally as you become less emotionally invested in your family's behavior and more focused on your own life and relationships.

Life Changes: Major life events like having children, facing serious illness, or experiencing loss may shift your perspective on forgiveness in unexpected ways.

There's no timeline for any of this, and you may move back and forth between different stages. All of this is normal and healthy.

Healing Exercises

Reflection Prompts

Take your time with these questions. Write your answers in your journal or notebook, and remember that your responses may change over time.

- *Your Forgiveness History:* What were you taught about forgiveness growing up? How has this information served or harmed you?
- *Current Beliefs:* How do you define forgiveness now? How is this different from what you were taught?
- *Pressure Assessment:* Who in your life is pressuring you to forgive? How does this pressure affect you?
- *Emotional Check-in:* What emotions come up when you think about forgiving specific family members? All emotions are valid.
- *Healing Priorities:* What would you most want to focus on in your healing—forgiveness, acceptance, growth, justice, or something else?
- *Benefits Analysis:* What benefits, if any, might forgiveness offer you personally? What risks might it pose?
- *Alternative Paths:* If not forgiveness, what other approaches to healing feel right for you?
- *Self-Compassion:* In what ways do you need to forgive yourself for how you coped with family trauma?
- *Boundary Connections:* How does your thinking about forgiveness affect your boundary decisions?
- *Future Visioning:* How do you hope your relationship with forgiveness might evolve as you continue healing?

The Forgiveness Exploration Letter

This is an expanded version of the forgiveness letter exercise, designed to help you explore all aspects of your relationship with forgiveness.

Part 1: To the Person Who Hurt You (Remember, you will never send this)

- Write about specific incidents and their impact
- Express all your emotions without censoring
- Describe how their behavior affected your life
- Share what you wish had been different
- Express what you need them to understand

Part 2: To Yourself

- Acknowledge your pain and struggles
- Give yourself permission to feel your feelings
- Recognize your strength and resilience
- Offer yourself compassion for how you coped
- Give yourself permission to heal at your own pace
- Commit to treating yourself with kindness

Part 3: To Your Future Self

- Share your hopes for your healing journey
- Describe the person you're becoming
- Offer encouragement for challenges ahead
- Express confidence in your ability to heal
- Commit to honoring your own needs and boundaries

Self-Affirmations for Forgiveness and Healing

Use these affirmations daily, or create your own that feel more authentic to your experience.

- "My healing journey is valid exactly as it is."
- "I have the right to forgive or not forgive as it serves my well-being."
- "I have the right to feel my feelings without having to justify them to others."
- "I release the need to carry anger that no longer serves me."
- "I can acknowledge harm without being consumed by resentment."
- "I have the right to set my own boundaries without having to justify them to anyone."
- "I have the right to change my boundaries as my needs change."
- "My worth is not dependent on forgiving those who hurt me."

- "I trust myself to know what I need for healing."
- "I choose thoughts and actions that serve my highest good."
- "I am free to change my mind about forgiveness as I grow."
- "My healing serves not only me but future generations."
- "I deserve peace, regardless of whether others seek forgiveness."

The Release Ritual

You can choose how to let go and take care of yourself — counseling, medication if you need it, meditating, yoga, martial arts to protect yourself, herbal remedies, a spiritual retreat, etc. — the possibilities are endless!

Create your own ritual for releasing what no longer serves you. This might involve:

Writing and Burning: Write down resentments, anger, or pain on paper and safely burn them while setting intentions for release. What you write doesn't have to be formal or even make sense. You can just write what comes to mind at the moment.

Water Ceremony: Write on water-soluble paper and watch your words dissolve in a stream, lake, or bathtub. Using children's bathtub crayons is great to write on the side of the tub while you're sitting in a warm, relaxing bath.

Burial Ritual: Bury written words or symbolic objects while planting something new in the same soil.

Movement Release: Use dance, martial arts, or vigorous exercise to physically release trapped emotions.

Art Expression: Create art that represents your pain and then transform it into something that represents your healing.

Meditation Practice: Develop a regular meditation practice focused on releasing what doesn't serve you and cultivating peace.

The key is choosing or creating something that feels meaningful and authentic to you.

Moving Forward

As you continue your healing journey, remember that forgiveness—or the choice not to forgive—is just one tool among many. You have the choice to look at your life and change it — walk away, with peace. What matters most is not whether you forgive your toxic family members, but whether you're able to free yourself from the power their past actions have over your present life.

Some days you may feel forgiving, others you may feel angry, and still others you may feel indifferent. All of these responses are valid and healthy. Healing isn't about achieving a permanent state of forgiveness or transcendence—it's about developing the flexibility to feel your emotions fully without being controlled by them.

Your journey toward peace and freedom is uniquely yours. Trust yourself to know what you need, when you need it, and how to honor your own healing process. Whether that includes forgiveness or not, you deserve to live a life free from the toxic patterns that once defined your family relationships.

It's equally ok to not know what you need at the moment. Trust that you will know what is right for you when the time comes.

Chapter 6: Grieving the Loss of Someone Still Alive

There's a unique and profound grief that comes with distancing yourself from toxic family members—a grief that society rarely acknowledges or validates. Unlike death, where finality marks the start of mourning, this kind of loss lingers in an in-between space. The person is still alive, still in the world, but they're no longer part of your life in the way they once were. This creates a complex emotional landscape that can feel isolating and confusing, especially when others don't understand why you're grieving someone who is "still here."

This chapter explores the paradox of loving someone while needing distance from them, the process of mourning relationships that may have never truly existed, and the difficult work of accepting that some people may never change. We'll examine how to hold space for your grief while honoring your truth and protecting your well-being.

The Paradox of Love and Distance

One of the most challenging aspects of cutting ties with toxic family members is the reality that love and harm can coexist. You may deeply love your mother, father, sibling, or other family member while simultaneously recognizing that their presence in your life causes significant damage to your mental health and well-being. This creates an internal conflict that can feel impossible to resolve.

Society tells us that love should conquer all, that if we truly love someone, we should be willing to endure anything they put us through. This messaging is particularly strong when it comes to family relationships, where we're taught that "blood is thicker than water" and that family members deserve endless chances to hurt us because they "love us in their own way."

The reality is more complex. Love is not always enough to sustain a healthy relationship. Love without respect, boundaries, and emotional safety becomes a prison rather than a gift. You can love someone deeply while acknowledging that they are harmful to you. You can honor the positive aspects of your relationship while still choosing to protect yourself from the negative ones.

This paradox often creates intense guilt. You may find yourself questioning whether your love was ever real if you're able to walk away. You might wonder if you're being selfish or cruel by prioritizing your well-being over the relationship. These feelings are normal and valid, but they don't mean you're making the wrong choice. You need to make the choice that is best for you!

Love, in its truest form, includes self-love and self-respect. When we allow ourselves to be repeatedly harmed in the name of love, we're actually dishonoring the concept entirely. Healthy love requires mutual respect, emotional safety, and the ability to maintain your authentic self within the relationship. When these elements are consistently absent, the most loving thing you can do is to create distance.

It's important to recognize that choosing distance doesn't erase the love you feel. The love remains, but it exists now in a different form, one that prioritizes your well-being over maintaining a harmful relationship. This is not a lesser form of love; it's a mature, boundaried love that recognizes the difference between enabling and truly caring for someone.

Mourning the Fantasy, Not the Reality

Perhaps the most complicated aspect of grieving toxic family relationships is recognizing that you're often mourning relationships that never truly existed in the way you hoped. You're grieving the fantasy of the loving, supportive parent, the relationship with the sibling who truly saw and accepted you, or the grandparent who provided unconditional love and wisdom. There is the loss of a dream of what the relationship could have been.

These fantasies aren't silly or unrealistic. They're natural human longings for connection, belonging, and love. Every child deserves to feel safe, seen, and valued. When this doesn't happen, we often spend years trying to make it happen, holding onto hope that someday our family members will become who we need them to be.

The grief for these fantasy relationships can be more intense than grieving the actual relationships because it encompasses all the dreams, hopes, and expectations you've carried. You're not just mourning what was lost; you're mourning what never was and never will be. This brings the loss of what could have been, coupled with the knowledge of what is unattainable.

This type of grief often comes in waves throughout your life. You might feel it acutely when you see other families interacting with warmth and respect, during holidays when the absence of healthy family connection feels most pronounced, or during major life events when you wish you had family members to share your joy or provide support.

It's crucial to allow yourself to grieve these fantasy relationships fully. Don't minimize your pain by telling yourself that you're mourning something that "wasn't real." The hopes and dreams were real, even if the relationships never lived up to them. The love you were prepared to give was real, even if it wasn't received in the way you hoped. The vision you had of family connection was real, even if it was never reciprocated.

Estrangement grief carries a unique weight because, unlike death, it lives in silence, unrecognized and unsupported by a society that expects family ties to remain unbroken. People may tell you to "focus on the positive" or remind you that "at least they're still alive." These responses, while often well-meaning, fail to acknowledge the legitimate loss you're experiencing.

Allow yourself to mourn not just what was, but what could have been in a different reality. Grieve the mother-daughter shopping trips that never happened because your mother was too critical or competitive. Mourn the supportive relationship with your father that never developed because he was emotionally unavailable or abusive. Honor the sadness for the sibling friendship that never existed because of jealousy, manipulation, or triangulation by other family members.

The Ambiguous Loss

Psychologist Pauline Boss coined the term "ambiguous loss" to describe losses that lack clarity or closure. This perfectly describes the experience of distancing yourself from toxic family members. Unlike death, where there are rituals, social support, and a clear understanding that loss has occurred, this type of loss exists in a gray area. The person is still alive, but they're no longer part of your life in the way they once were. Full closure and moving forward can be more challenging when we know that one day we may meet that person again, we may hear about their lives from others, or see them on social media.

There's no funeral to attend, no casket to lower into the ground, no clear endpoint to mark the beginning of your mourning process. Instead, you're left with a persistent sense of loss that may ebb and flow without clear resolution.

This ambiguous nature can make the grief feel more complicated and prolonged. Without clear social recognition of your loss, you may find yourself grieving alone, questioning whether your feelings are valid. You might feel guilty for mourning someone who is still alive, or confused by the intensity of your emotions around a relationship you chose to end.

The ambiguity is compounded by the fact that the relationship may not be completely severed. You might still hear updates about your estranged family member through mutual connections, see their social media posts, or encounter them at family gatherings you both attend. These encounters can trigger fresh pain and reignite the grief process, making it challenging to achieve closure or peace.

It's worth noting that key family relationships are not only made up of exchanges of words and messages. Relationships between family members are energetic, emotional, and heart-centred connections, and we still have that shared history in the form of memories, however traumatic they may be. So we may take distance and space in terms of communication, but the 'cords' of the relationship may still exist. We may sense and feel their presence, which can hold us in the relationship even if we have ceased contact.

It's important to recognize that ambiguous loss is still loss, and it deserves the same respect and attention as more traditional forms of grief. Your feelings are valid even without a clear endpoint or social recognition. You have the right to mourn the end of these relationships in whatever way feels authentic to you.

Accepting That They May Never Change

One of the most difficult aspects of this grief process is accepting that the person you're distancing yourself from may never become the person you need them to be. This acceptance doesn't come easily, especially when you've spent years hoping, trying, and believing that change was possible.

We often stay in toxic relationships because we can see glimpses of the person's potential. We remember the good moments, the times when they seemed to understand, the brief periods when the relationship felt healthy and supportive. These glimpses fuel hope that permanent change is possible, that if we just try hard enough or love enough or explain ourselves clearly enough, they'll finally become the person we need them to be.

Accepting that change may not happen requires grieving your role as the person responsible for their growth or healing. Many of us take on the burden of trying to fix, heal, or change our family members, believing that our love and persistence will eventually break through their defenses or dysfunction. Letting go of this role can feel like giving up on them, which can trigger guilt and sadness.

The reality is that people change when they want to change, when they're ready to change, and when they're willing to do the difficult work that change requires. You cannot love someone into health, argue them into self-awareness, or sacrifice your well-being to motivate their growth. Change is an inside job that requires acknowledgment, accountability, and sustained effort from the person themselves.

This doesn't mean you were wrong to hope or try. It means you're recognizing the limits of your influence and accepting the reality of the situation as it currently exists. This acceptance is not defeat; it's wisdom. It's the recognition that your energy is better spent on your own healing and growth rather than trying to change someone who may not be willing to put in the work required to change.

Accepting that they may never change also means grieving the future you imagined with them. You may have envisioned family gatherings where everyone gets along, holidays filled with warmth and connection, or milestone celebrations where your family member shows up with love and support. Letting go of these future fantasies is part of the grieving process.

The Waves of Grief

Grief in toxic family estrangement does not move in a straight line. It is often referred to as a *living loss*, because the relationship is gone even though the person still remains. The emotions and stages of healing in estrangement frequently parallel those experienced after a death, though with added layers of complexity. You won't move through it in neat stages that build upon each other toward resolution. Instead, grief comes in waves that can catch you off guard, sometimes long after you thought you had processed the loss.

These waves might be triggered by specific events: seeing a healthy family interaction in public, watching a movie that depicts the kind of family relationship you always wanted, or reaching a milestone that you wish you could share with them. They might also arise seemingly out of nowhere, during ordinary moments when you're reminded of their absence in your life. Grief is a funny thing. It comes in waves when you least expect it.

The intensity of these waves can be surprising and overwhelming. You might find yourself crying in the grocery store because you pass their favorite food, or feeling a deep sadness while watching a commercial that reminds you of happier times. These responses are normal and don't indicate that you're not healing or that you made the wrong decision.

It's important to allow these waves to pass through you without judgment. Don't try to stop the tears, suppress the sadness, or talk yourself out of feeling the loss. Grief has its own timeline and rhythm, and fighting against it often prolongs the process.

Some waves will be bigger than others. Anniversaries, holidays, and family milestones may bring particularly intense grief. The first Christmas after going no contact, your birthday without their call, or Mother's Day or Father's Day when you're not speaking, can feel overwhelming. Plan for these difficult times by ensuring you have extra support, engaging in self-care activities, and being gentle with yourself.

Other waves might be smaller but persistent—a low-level sadness that accompanies you through ordinary days, a sense of emptiness during family-oriented events, or a longing that surfaces when you see other people enjoying healthy family relationships.

Remember that experiencing these waves doesn't mean you're not healing or that you should reconsider your boundaries. Grief is a testament to the significance of the relationship and the depth of your caring. You can miss someone while still knowing that distance is necessary for your well-being.

Disenfranchised Grief

Your grief for toxic family relationships may not be recognized or validated by others in your life, making it what psychologists call "disenfranchised grief." Society has clear scripts for mourning death, divorce, or job loss, but there's no roadmap for grieving the loss of living family members. Many do not understand, so it can feel isolating.

Friends and extended family members may not understand why you're sad about ending a relationship that they witnessed as harmful. They might offer unhelpful advice like "But they're your family; you should have talked to them", or guilt trips such as "Why are you sad? You didn't talk to them anyway." To someone who has never been estranged, it's impossible to understand.

Some people in your life may even be threatened by your decision to distance yourself from toxic family members because it challenges their own tolerance for dysfunction or forces them to examine their own family relationships. They may pressure you to reconcile or minimize your reasons for creating distance, which can complicate your grief.

This lack of social validation can make you question whether your grief is appropriate or proportionate. You might wonder if you're being dramatic, if you should just "get over it," or if you're making a bigger deal out of the loss than necessary. These doubts can prevent you from fully processing your emotions and healing from the relationship.

It's crucial to seek out people who can validate your experience and support your grief process. You do not owe anyone an explanation for these feelings, nor do you need permission to feel them. During your grieving process, choose to spend time with those who validate you and your feelings. This might include friends who have gone through similar experiences, support groups for people from dysfunctional families, or therapists who understand family trauma. Having even one person who truly gets what you're going through can make an enormous difference in your healing process.

Online communities can also provide valuable support and validation. Many people find comfort in connecting with others who have made similar decisions about toxic family members. These communities can offer understanding, practical advice, and the reminder that you're not alone in your experience.

Honoring Your Truth While Grieving

Grieving toxic family relationships requires holding two seemingly contradictory truths simultaneously: you can miss someone deeply while knowing that distance from them is necessary for your well-being. This both/and thinking can feel uncomfortable, especially in a culture that prefers simple, either/or explanations for complex situations. You might feel guilt that you never got the chance to mend what was broken one moment, then find yourself feeling a wave of relief that you no longer have to hold out hope for resolution. You might witness your own anger, sorrow, and even happiness existing side-by-side and wonder how that could even be. Your emotions can and will co-exist; there is no room for "should" in the emotional experience.

You might feel guilty for missing someone who hurt you, or confused by feeling sad about a relationship that was largely negative. These mixed emotions are normal and don't indicate confusion or lack of resolve. They indicate the complex nature of human relationships and the capacity to hold multiple feelings at once.

Honoring your truth means accepting all of your feelings about the relationship without judgment. You can acknowledge the good memories while not minimizing the harm that occurred. You can feel grateful for positive experiences while still maintaining boundaries that protect you from negative ones. You can love someone while choosing not to have them in your life.

This honoring might involve creating rituals or practices that acknowledge your grief while affirming your choice to prioritize your well-being. It's okay to feel your grief. It's also okay not to feel anything at all. These feelings can also coexist. You might write letters that you never send, create photo albums that capture positive memories, or engage in activities that help you process your emotions in healthy ways.

Some people find it helpful to have conversations with the person they're grieving, either through journaling, talking to an empty chair, or imagining what they would say if they had the opportunity. These practices can help you express feelings that you may not have been able to communicate while the relationship was active.

It's also important to honor your truth by not rushing the grief process or allowing others to dictate how long you should take to "get over it." Grief has its own timeline, and healing happens at different rates for different people. There is no timeline for anyone to heal. There's no prescribed schedule for mourning the loss of toxic family relationships.

Creating New Meanings and Connections

Part of grieving toxic family relationships involves creating new meanings around family and belonging. When your biological family doesn't provide the love, support, and connection you need, you have the ability to create chosen family relationships that do meet these needs.

This doesn't mean replacing your biological family with substitutes, but rather expanding your definition of family to include people who treat you with the love, respect, and acceptance you deserve. Chosen family might include close friends, mentors, romantic partners, or community members who show up for you in ways your biological family can't or won't.

Creating chosen family relationships takes time and intention. It requires learning to recognize healthy relationship patterns, developing trust with new people, and allowing yourself to be vulnerable with those who have earned that privilege. This process can feel scary, especially if you're coming from relationships where vulnerability was met with manipulation or harm.

From the grief of toxic family relationships, you may find new wisdom that helps you build healthier connections. Having experienced what doesn't work in relationships can help you recognize and appreciate what does work. You may find yourself more sensitive to red flags, more appreciative of genuine kindness, and more committed to maintaining healthy boundaries in new relationships.

Some people find meaning in their experience by helping others who are going through similar struggles. This might involve volunteering with organizations that support people from dysfunctional families, sharing your story to help others feel less alone, or simply being a supportive presence for friends who are dealing with similar family dynamics. For me, writing this book is a way to help others going through similar situations.

Finding new meanings doesn't erase the grief, but it can help you understand that your experience has value and purpose beyond the pain it caused. Your journey toward health and healing can become a source of wisdom, strength, and connection with others who need to know that healing is possible and is as individual as each person.

Grief as a Gateway to Healing

While grief for toxic family relationships can feel overwhelming and endless, it's actually a crucial part of the healing process. Grief is how we integrate loss and find ways to continue living authentically despite what we've lost. It's the emotional work that allows us to create space for new experiences and relationships.

Avoiding or suppressing grief often prolongs the healing process and can lead to other problems like depression, anxiety, or difficulty forming new relationships. By allowing yourself to fully experience and express your grief, you're doing the necessary work to heal from the relationship and create space for healthier connections in your life.

Grief also helps you clarify your values and priorities. Going through the process of mourning toxic family relationships often helps people understand what they truly need and want in relationships. It can strengthen your commitment to maintaining boundaries, increase your appreciation for healthy relationships, and deepen your understanding of your own worth and deserving of love.

The process of grieving can also lead to positive changes that can emerge from struggling with difficult life experiences. Many people who have grieved toxic family relationships report increased empathy, stronger relationships with chosen family, clearer personal values, deeper appreciation for life, and increased confidence in their ability to handle challenges. Yet, we do heal, and it is the gradual realization that we will survive the loss that makes working on ourselves so transforming.

Reflection: How to Hold Space for Your Grief and Honor Your Truth

As you work through the complex emotions of grieving someone who is still alive, use these reflection prompts and exercises to help you honor your experience and find your path forward.

Self-Reflection Questions

Understanding Your Grief:

- What aspects of this relationship am I actually grieving?
- How does my grief for this living person compare to other losses I've experienced?
- What makes this particular loss feel complicated or confusing?
- In what ways has society's messaging about family affected how I view my grief?

Exploring Your Emotions:

- What contradictory emotions am I experiencing about this person and this loss?
- How do I feel when people tell me I shouldn't be sad about someone who is "still alive"?

- What would I want people to understand about my experience of this loss?
- How has this grief changed or evolved over time?

Honoring Your Truth:

- What positive memories do I want to honor about this relationship?
- What harmful aspects am I glad to no longer experience?
- How can I hold both love and boundaries simultaneously?
- What would it mean to truly accept that this person may never change?

Grief Mapping Exercise

Create a visual map of your grief by drawing or writing responses to these prompts:

Center Circle: Write the name of the person you're grieving

Inner Ring: List what you're actually grieving (the fantasy relationship, specific hopes, future possibilities)

Middle Ring: Identify your complex emotions (love, anger, relief, sadness, guilt, peace)

Outer Ring: Note your support systems and coping strategies

Letter to Your Grief

Write a letter to your grief, acknowledging its presence and purpose in your life.

"Dear Grief,

I see you and I acknowledge that you belong here because..."

"You've taught me..."

"What I need from you right now is..."

"What I want you to know is..."

Creating Meaning Ritual

Design a personal ritual to honor both the relationship that was and your choice to prioritize your well-being.

- Light a candle for what you're grateful for and what you're releasing
- Create a memory box with positive mementos and a letter explaining your boundaries

- Plant something in your garden to represent growth
- Donate to a cause that helps people from dysfunctional families
- Write in a journal about how this experience has made you stronger or wiser

Waves of Grief Tracking

For one month, note when grief waves occur:

- What triggered the wave?
- How intense was it (1-10 scale)?
- How long did it last?
- What helped you through it?
- What did you learn about your grief patterns?

Affirmations for Complex Grief

Practice these affirmations when you need to validate your experience:

- "My grief is valid even though this person is still alive"
- "I can love someone and still need distance from them"
- "My feelings are complex because relationships are complex"
- "I deserve to mourn the family relationships I never had"
- "Healing doesn't require reconciliation"
- "My chosen family is just as real and valuable as biological family"
- "I am breaking generational cycles by prioritizing my well-being"
- "Grief is the price of having cared deeply"

The Both/And Practice

When you notice yourself caught in either/or thinking about your grief, practice both/and statements:

Instead of: "I shouldn't be sad because they hurt me"

Try: "I can feel sad about losing them AND relieved to be free from their toxicity"

Instead of: "I either loved them or I didn't"

Try: "I can love who they could have been AND accept who they actually were"

Instead of: "I should either reconcile or completely forget them"

Try: "I can honor positive memories AND maintain protective boundaries"

Moving Forward Visioning

Write about or draw your vision for moving forward:

- What does healing look like for you?
- How do you want to honor this relationship while protecting your well-being?
- What kind of family relationships do you want to create or nurture?
- How can this experience help with your future choices about relationships?
- What wisdom have you gained that you can share with others?

Remember, grieving someone who is still alive is one of the most complex emotional experiences a person can have. Be patient with yourself, honor all of your feelings, and trust that healing is possible even when the path isn't clear. Your grief is valid, your boundaries are necessary, and your healing matters.

Chapter 7: Rewriting the Narrative of Who You Are

Growing up in a toxic family system doesn't just affect your relationships—it fundamentally shapes how you see yourself. The messages you have received about your worth, your capabilities, and your place in the world become internalized as core beliefs that can follow you long after you've left the harmful environment. These beliefs often masquerade as truth, whispering that you're not good enough, that you don't deserve love, or that you're fundamentally flawed in some way.

But here's what toxic families don't want you to know: the story they told you about who you are was never the truth. It was a narrative constructed to serve their dysfunction, to keep you small, compliant, and available for their emotional needs. The real you—the authentic, worthy, capable you—has always existed beneath the layers of false programming they imposed.

This chapter is about reclaiming your true identity and rewriting the story of who you are. It's about recognizing the difference between who you were forced to become for survival and who you actually are when you're free to be yourself. We'll explore how to deconstruct the false identities imposed on you, reconnect with your authentic self, and learn to trust the positive feedback from people who actually see and value you.

Deconstructing False Identities

In toxic family systems, children aren't allowed to develop authentic identities based on their natural temperament, interests, and strengths. Instead, they're assigned roles and identities that serve the family's dysfunction. You might have been cast as the responsible one, the problem child, the mediator, the invisible one, or any number of other roles that had nothing to do with who you really were and everything to do with what the family needed from you.

These assigned identities often come with rigid rules and expectations. The "responsible one" must never need help or show vulnerability. The "problem child" becomes the repository for all the family's dysfunction and blame. The "peacemaker" must sacrifice their own needs to keep everyone else happy. The "golden child" must maintain perfection at all costs. The "invisible one" must never take up space or have needs.

Over time, these false identities become so ingrained that you may not even recognize them as having been constructed. You might genuinely believe that you are naturally anxious, inherently selfish, fundamentally flawed, or destined to fail. You might think these characteristics are just part of your personality rather than learned responses to a toxic environment.

The first step in reclaiming your authentic identity is recognizing these false narratives for what they are. Start by examining the core beliefs you hold about yourself. Ask yourself: Where did these beliefs come from? What evidence do I actually have for them? Are these beliefs based on my authentic experiences, or were they imposed on me by others?

Common false identities imposed by toxic families include:

The Overresponsible Child: You learned that your worth depended on taking care of everyone else's needs and emotions. You might struggle with the belief that you're selfish for having your own needs or that you're only valuable when you're useful to others.

The Scapegoat: You were blamed for the family's problems and may have internalized the belief that you're inherently bad, difficult, or the cause of conflict wherever you go.

The Perfect Child: You learned that love was conditional on performance and may struggle with perfectionism, fear of failure, and the belief that you're only worthwhile when you're achieving.

The Invisible Child: You learned to take up as little space as possible and may struggle with the belief that you don't matter, that your thoughts and feelings aren't important, or that you don't deserve attention or care.

The Emotional Caretaker: You became responsible for managing everyone else's emotions and may struggle with the belief that you're responsible for how other people feel and that conflict is always your fault.

The Problem Child: You were labeled as difficult or troubled and may have internalized the belief that you're inherently problematic, that you ruin everything, or that you don't deserve good things.

As you begin to recognize these false identities, you might experience grief for the authentic self that was never allowed to develop. You might find that you identify with more than one of these false identities. You might feel angry about the ways you were misunderstood or mischaracterized. These feelings are normal and important parts of the healing process. Allow yourself to feel them fully without judgment.

Uncovering Your Authentic Self

Beneath the layers of false programming lies your authentic self—the person you were meant to be before toxic family dynamics shaped you into your imposed identity. This authentic self has always been there, even when it was buried under survival mechanisms and imposed identities. Reconnecting with this true self is both a process of remembering and a process of discovery.

Start by thinking back to moments when you felt most like yourself. These might be times when you were alone and engaged in activities you genuinely enjoyed, moments when you felt truly seen and accepted by someone, or experiences where you felt fully alive and engaged. What were you doing? How were you different from who you were brought up to believe you were? What qualities did you express in these moments?

Pay attention to the activities, environments, and people that make you feel energized rather than drained. Your authentic self naturally gravitates toward what nourishes it and away from what depletes it. If you've spent years ignoring these natural preferences to please others or fit into imposed roles, you might need to relearn how to recognize and trust these internal signals.

Consider the qualities and characteristics that others have appreciated in you, particularly those that your family of origin twisted. Toxic families often twist what is healthy and reframe strengths as weaknesses. Qualities like sensitivity, independence, or assertiveness—traits that serve you well in the world—may be criticized, mocked, or treated as flaws within the family system. Over time, this can leave you questioning your worth and doubting the very qualities that make you resilient. Recognizing this pattern is an important step in reclaiming your truth: the problem was never your strength, but the way it was distorted by those unwilling to honor it.

Look for patterns in the feedback you receive from healthy, supportive people in your life. What do they consistently notice and appreciate about you? These observations from people who have no investment in keeping you small can provide valuable insight into your authentic qualities.

Your authentic self also includes your natural emotional responses, your genuine interests, your personal values, and your unique way of seeing the world. You might discover that you're naturally more extroverted or introverted than your family allowed you to be. You might find that you have interests or talents that were never encouraged or were actively discouraged. You might realize that your values differ significantly from those of your family of origin.

Remember that authenticity isn't about being perfect or having a completely developed sense of self right away. It's about being genuine, allowing yourself to be human, and giving yourself permission to grow and change. Your authentic self isn't a fixed identity that you need to discover once and for all—it's a dynamic, evolving aspect of who you are that continues to develop throughout your life.

The process of uncovering your authentic self can be both exciting and scary. You might feel guilty for being different from what your family expected or needed you to be. You might worry that your authentic self is somehow wrong or unacceptable. It might take you some time to accept what others are telling you they appreciate about you. These concerns are normal, but remember that your worth isn't dependent on fitting into anyone else's expectations or serving anyone else's needs.

Recognizing Your Survival Strategies

Much of what you might consider your "personality" may actually be composed of survival strategies you developed to navigate a toxic family environment. These strategies served an important purpose—they helped you survive emotionally, physically, or psychologically in circumstances that were beyond your control. However, they may no longer serve you in healthier environments and relationships.

Common survival strategies include people-pleasing, perfectionism, emotional numbness, hypervigilance, conflict avoidance, and taking responsibility for others' emotions. You might have learned to scan environments for signs of danger, to anticipate others' needs before your own, to minimize your own feelings, or to become whatever others needed you to be.

It's important to recognize these strategies with compassion rather than criticism. They weren't character flaws or weaknesses—they were intelligent adaptations to abnormal circumstances. The part of you that developed these strategies was trying to protect you and help you survive. However, as you create distance from toxic family dynamics and build healthier relationships, you may find that these strategies no longer serve you and may actually interfere with your ability to be authentic and connect genuinely with others.

For example, if you learned to be hypervigilant about others' moods and needs, you might find yourself exhausted in healthy relationships because you're still constantly monitoring and trying to manage everyone else's emotional state. If you learned to avoid conflict at all costs, you might struggle to advocate for yourself or address legitimate issues in your relationships.

The goal isn't to completely eliminate these strategies—some of them may continue to serve you in certain contexts—but rather to develop awareness of when you're using them and to create choices about when and how you employ them. You want to move from automatic, unconscious reactions to conscious, intentional responses.

Start by noticing when you're operating from survival mode versus when you're able to be more authentic and relaxed. What triggers the shift into survival strategies? What helps you return to a more authentic state? This awareness is the first step in developing the ability to choose different responses.

The Inner Critic and Family Voices

One of the most persistent legacies of toxic family dynamics is the internalized voice of criticism and judgment that continues to operate long after you've left the harmful environment. This inner critic often sounds like the voices of your toxic family members, repeating the same criticisms, judgments, and predictions of failure that you heard throughout your childhood and beyond.

The inner critic might tell you that you're being too sensitive when you feel hurt, that you're selfish when you prioritize your needs, that you're overreacting when you set boundaries, or that you don't deserve good things when opportunities arise. These voices can be so automatic and pervasive that you might not even recognize them as separate from your own thoughts.

Learning to identify and separate these internalized voices from your authentic thoughts and feelings is crucial for developing a healthy sense of self. Start by paying attention to the tone and content of your internal dialogue. Does it sound supportive and encouraging, or critical and harsh? Does it reflect the kind of compassion you would show a good friend, or does it echo the judgment and criticism you experienced in your family?

71

When you notice critical or judgmental thoughts, ask yourself: Whose voice does this sound like? Is this something I would say to someone I care about? Is this thought helpful or harmful? Does this belief serve me, or does it keep me small and stuck?

You can begin to challenge these internalized voices by developing a more compassionate, supportive internal dialogue. This might feel artificial at first, especially if you're not used to treating yourself with kindness. Start small, perhaps by simply noticing when you're being self-critical and gently redirecting your attention to something more loving and compassionate.

Some people find it helpful to imagine what a loving, supportive person would say to them in challenging moments. Others create a more nurturing internal voice by consciously practicing self-compassion and encouragement. Over time, these new patterns of internal dialogue can become more natural and automatic.

Remember that changing these deeply ingrained patterns takes time and patience. You've probably been practicing self-criticism for many years, so it will take time to develop new habits of self-compassion. Be gentle with yourself in this process and celebrate your small victories along the way.

Learning to Trust Positive Feedback

One of the most challenging aspects of rewriting your narrative is learning to believe positive feedback from others. When you've been consistently criticized, blamed, or made to feel inadequate, genuine praise or appreciation can feel foreign, uncomfortable, or even suspicious. You might automatically dismiss compliments, assume people are just being nice, or worry that they don't really know the "real" you.

This difficulty accepting positive feedback isn't about humility or modesty; it's about the way toxic family dynamics damage your ability to see yourself accurately. You may find accepting positive feedback is difficult at first, but it will get easier in time.

When the people who were supposed to love and support you unconditionally instead consistently focused on your flaws and failings, it created a distorted lens through which you view yourself.

Learning to trust positive feedback is a gradual process that requires conscious effort and practice. Start by noticing your automatic responses to compliments or positive observations. Do you immediately deflect or dismiss them? Do you feel uncomfortable or suspicious? Do you assume the person must be mistaken or doesn't really know you?

Instead of automatically rejecting positive feedback, try to pause and consider it more carefully. Ask yourself: Is there any truth to what this person is saying? Can I allow for the possibility that they see something in me that I don't see in myself? What would it mean if their positive perception of me were accurate?

It can be helpful to keep a record of positive feedback you receive from people you trust and respect. Write down the specific things people say they appreciate about you, the compliments you receive, and the positive observations others make about your character or abilities. When your inner critic is particularly active, you can refer back to this record as evidence of your actual worth and value.

Pay particular attention to feedback from people who have no obvious reason to lie to you or flatter you. These might be colleagues who appreciate your work, friends who value your friendship, or even strangers who benefit from your kindness or competence. The consistency of positive feedback from various sources over time can help you begin to see yourself more accurately. You can also say these positive things to yourself daily, which can help you start seeing these things in yourself.

Remember that people who truly care about you want to see you succeed and feel good about yourself. Their positive feedback isn't manipulation or false flattery—it's their genuine perception of your value and worth. Learning to receive and believe this feedback is an act of healing and a step toward developing a more accurate and compassionate view of yourself.

Developing Your Own Voice and Opinions

In toxic family systems, having your own thoughts, feelings, and opinions is often discouraged or punished. You might have learned that disagreeing with family members led to conflict, criticism, rejection, or punishment. You might have been told that your thoughts weren't important, your feelings were wrong, or your opinions didn't matter. Over time, you may have stopped forming your own opinions altogether, instead automatically adopting whatever seemed safest or most acceptable.

Developing your authentic voice and your own opinions is a crucial part of reclaiming your identity. This process might feel uncomfortable or even scary at first, especially if you've spent years suppressing your authentic thoughts and feelings. You might not even know what you really think about various topics because you've become so accustomed to deferring to others.

Start by paying attention to your gut reactions to different situations, ideas, or experiences. Before you consider what others might think or what the "right" response might be, notice what your initial, uncensored reaction is. This gut response often contains valuable information about your authentic thoughts and feelings.

Practice forming opinions on low-stakes topics first. What kind of music do you genuinely enjoy? What foods do you actually prefer? What activities make you feel energized versus drained? What types of movies or books do you find interesting? These might seem like trivial questions, but they're important building blocks for developing your authentic voice.

As you become more comfortable expressing opinions on smaller matters, you can gradually work up to more significant issues. What are your values? What do you believe about relationships, work, parenting, or other important life areas? What kind of life do you want to create for yourself?

It's important to remember that having your own opinions doesn't mean you have to express them in every situation or that you need to argue with anyone who disagrees with you. Part of developing your authentic voice is also developing the wisdom to know when and how to share your thoughts and when it might be more appropriate to keep them to yourself.

You also don't need to have strong opinions about everything. It's perfectly okay to be uncertain, to change your mind, or to hold nuanced views that don't fit neatly into any particular category. Your authentic voice includes your doubts, your evolving thoughts, and your willingness to learn and grow.

Rewriting Your Story

Once you've begun to deconstruct your false identities, uncover your authentic self, and develop your own voice, you can start the process of consciously rewriting your narrative. This isn't about denying or minimizing the impact of your experiences—

it's about placing those experiences in a broader context that includes your resilience, growth, and capacity for healing.

Your new narrative should acknowledge the challenges you've faced while also recognizing your strength in surviving them. It should honor your pain while also celebrating your courage in choosing healing. It should include the ways you've been hurt while also recognizing your capacity for love, growth, and positive change.

This new story isn't about becoming perfect or pretending that your past doesn't matter. It's about creating a more complete, accurate, and empowering understanding of who you are. Instead of seeing yourself as permanently damaged or defined by your trauma, you can begin to see yourself as someone who has overcome significant challenges and is continuing to grow and heal.

Your rewritten narrative might include themes like resilience, courage, wisdom gained through difficulty, the ability to break generational cycles, and the capacity for authentic love and connection. These stories validate your pain while celebrating your strength and transformation.

For example, instead of "I'm damaged because I grew up in a toxic family," you might develop a narrative like "I survived a difficult childhood and have developed remarkable strength, empathy, and wisdom as a result. I'm breaking generational cycles and creating a healthier life for myself and others."

Instead of "I'm bad at relationships because of my family," you might reframe it as "I'm learning to build healthy relationships despite not having good models in my family of origin. My experience with dysfunction helps me recognize and appreciate genuine love and respect."

This process of rewriting your story is ongoing and evolving. As you continue to heal and grow, your understanding of yourself and your experiences will deepen and change. Allow your narrative to be flexible and dynamic, able to incorporate new insights and experiences as they arise.

Creating New Patterns and Habits

Rewriting your narrative isn't just about changing how you think about yourself; it's also about creating new patterns of behavior that reflect your authentic self and support your continued growth. The habits and patterns you developed to survive in a toxic environment may not serve you in healthier contexts, and you may need to consciously develop new ways of being in the world.

This might include developing new patterns of self-care, learning to express your needs and boundaries clearly, practicing authentic communication, and choosing activities and relationships that align with your values and interests. It might also include breaking old patterns of people-pleasing, perfectionism, or emotional numbing that no longer serve you.

Creating new patterns requires conscious effort and practice. You're essentially rewiring neural pathways that have been reinforced for years or decades. Be patient with yourself as you develop these new habits, and expect some setbacks along the way. Change moves in cycles, not straight lines. At times of stress, you may find yourself returning to old patterns, but each return offers a chance to deepen your healing rather than erase it.

Focus on small, sustainable changes rather than trying to transform everything at once. Choose one or two new patterns to work on at a time, and give yourself several weeks or months to establish them before adding additional changes. This approach is more likely to create lasting transformation than trying to change everything simultaneously.

Building Your Support System

As you work to rewrite your narrative and develop your authentic self, it's crucial to surround yourself with people who can see and support the real you. This might include friends who appreciate your authentic qualities, mentors who encourage your growth, therapists who provide professional guidance, or support groups where you can connect with others who have had similar experiences.

Building a healthy support system after growing up in a toxic family can be challenging. You might struggle with trust, have difficulty recognizing healthy relationship patterns, or feel unsure about how to form genuine connections. These challenges are normal and understandable given your experiences.

Start by identifying people in your life who consistently treat you with respect, kindness, and genuine care. These might be friends, colleagues, neighbors, or even acquaintances who demonstrate healthy relationship skills. Pay attention to how you feel when you're with these people. Do you feel accepted for who you are? Do you feel energized rather than drained? Do they encourage your growth and celebrate your successes?

As you identify healthy relationships, invest more time and energy in nurturing them. This might mean being more vulnerable, sharing more of your authentic self, or simply spending more time together. Remember that healthy relationships are reciprocal—you should both give and receive support, encouragement, and genuine care.

You might also need to distance yourself from people who reinforce old patterns or make you feel worse about yourself. This can be particularly challenging if these are family members or long-term friends, but remember that protecting your healing and growth is not selfish—it's necessary.

Consider joining support groups, either in person or online, where you can connect with others who have had similar experiences with toxic family dynamics. These connections can provide validation, practical advice, and the reminder that you're not alone in your journey.

Integrating Your New Identity

As you develop a clearer sense of your authentic self and begin to rewrite your narrative, you'll face the ongoing challenge of integrating this new identity into all areas of your life. This integration process can be exciting but also disorienting, especially if you've spent years operating from false identities or survival strategies.

You might find that your new understanding of yourself creates some tension in existing relationships, particularly with people who were comfortable with your old patterns. Some people might resist your changes, especially if your growth challenges them to examine their own patterns or if they benefited from your previous people-pleasing or overgiving behaviors.

This resistance from others can be discouraging, but it's also a sign that you're making real changes. Not everyone will be supportive of your growth, and that's okay. Your healing and authenticity are worth more than maintaining relationships that require you to stay small and unhealthy.

In some cases, you might need to have explicit conversations with people about the changes you're making. This might involve setting new boundaries, expressing needs you've never voiced before, or simply showing up differently in the relationship. These conversations can be challenging, but they're often necessary for creating more authentic connections.

Be patient with yourself as you navigate this integration process. It takes time to fully embody a new way of being, and you might find yourself occasionally falling back into old patterns, especially during times of stress or conflict. This is normal and doesn't mean you're not making progress.

Remember that change is an ongoing process. As you continue to grow and heal, your understanding of yourself will continue to evolve. Allow yourself the flexibility to keep learning, changing, and becoming more authentically yourself throughout your life.

Reflection: Identifying and Rewriting Your Narrative

Use these exercises and reflection prompts to help you identify false identities, uncover your authentic self, and begin rewriting your story in a more empowering way.

Identifying False Identities

Family Role Analysis:

- What role or roles did you play in your family of origin?
- What were the spoken and unspoken expectations that came with this role?
- How did this role serve the family system? What problems did it solve or dysfunction did it enable?
- What aspects of your authentic self did you have to suppress to fulfill this role?
- How does this role still show up in your adult relationships and life?

Core Beliefs Examination:

Write down your immediate, uncensored answers to these prompts, then examine where these beliefs originated:

- I am...
- People always...
- I deserve...
- Love means...
- Conflict means...

- Success means...
- I should always...
- I should never…
- I am allowed to…

For each belief, ask yourself:

- Where did this belief come from?
- Whose voice does this sound like?
- What evidence do I have that this belief is true?
- How does this belief serve me or limit me?
- What would I believe instead if given the choice?

Uncovering Your Authentic Self

Authentic Moments Inventory:

Think of times when you felt most like yourself—energized, alive, and genuine. For each memory, reflect on:

- What were you doing?
- Who were you with?
- What environment were you in?
- What qualities were you expressing?
- How did you feel in your body?
- What made this moment feel so authentic?

Energy Audit: Create two lists:

1. Activities/Situations That Energize Me
2. Activities/Situations That Drain Me

Look for patterns. What themes do you notice? How might these patterns reflect your authentic preferences and needs?

Values Clarification:

From the list below, circle your top 10 values, then narrow it down to your top 5:

Adventure	Humility	Patriotism
Authenticity	Independence	Peace
Authority	Influence	Pleasure
Autonomy	Inner Harmony	Popularity
Beauty	Integrity	Power
Challenge	Intelligence	Recognition
Community	Intimacy	Relationships
Compassion	Joy	Religion
Competence	Justice	Reputation
Competition	Knowledge	Respect
Connection	Leadership	Responsibility
Creativity	Learning	Security
Excellence	Legacy	Service
Faith	Leisure	Spirituality
Fame	Love	Stability
Family	Loyalty	Success
Freedom	Meaningful Work	Tradition
Fun	Money	Travel
Growth	Nature	Truth
Health	Order	Wealth
Honesty	Parenting	Wisdom
Hope	Patience	

Reflection questions:

- How do your top values differ from your family's values?
- In what ways have you been living according to others' values rather than your own?
- How might you align your life more closely with your authentic values?

Recognizing Survival Strategies

Survival Strategy Assessment:

For each strategy below, rate how much you rely on it (1 = never, 5 = constantly):

- People-pleasing ___
- Perfectionism ___
- Emotional numbing ___
- Hypervigilance ___
- Conflict avoidance ___
- Over-responsibility for others ___
- Self-criticism ___
- Minimizing your needs ___
- Anticipating rejection ___
- Controlling outcomes ___

For your highest-rated strategies, reflect on:

- When did you first develop this strategy?
- How did it help you survive your family environment?
- How does it show up in your adult life?
- When does it serve you, and when does it limit you?
- What would you do differently if you felt completely safe?

Challenging the Inner Critic

Voice Identification Exercise:

For one week, pay attention to your internal dialogue. When you notice critical or harsh thoughts, write them down and ask:

- Whose voice does this sound like?
- Is this something my [mother/father/sibling] would say?

- Is this thought helpful or harmful?
- What would I say to a good friend in this situation?
- What would a loving, supportive voice say instead?

Compassionate Reframe Practice:

Take three of your harshest self-criticisms and rewrite them with compassion:

Critical thought: _____

Compassionate reframe: _____

Critical thought: _____

Compassionate reframe: _____

Critical thought: _____

Compassionate reframe: _____

Rewriting Your Story

Before and After Narratives:

Old Story (How I used to see myself):

Write a paragraph describing how you used to think about yourself, your capabilities, and your worth.

New Story (How I choose to see myself now):

Write a new paragraph that acknowledges your challenges while also recognizing your strength, growth, and potential.

Strength Inventory:

List 10 strengths you've developed as a result of your experiences:

1.
2.
3.
4.
5.
6.
7.
8.

9.

10.

Future Self Visualization:

Imagine yourself five years from now, living authentically and feeling confident in who you are:

- What does this future version of you do differently?
- How do they treat themselves?
- What relationships do they have?
- What values guide their decisions?
- What would they want to tell you right now?

Daily Practices for Identity Integration

Morning Identity Affirmation:

Choose 3-5 affirmations that reflect your authentic self and new narrative. Say them each morning:

- I am worthy of love and respect exactly as I am
- I trust my own perceptions and feelings
- I have the right to my own thoughts and opinions
- I am breaking generational patterns with courage and wisdom
- I attract people who appreciate my authentic self

Evening Reflection:

Each night, briefly reflect on:

- When did I feel most authentic today?
- When did I operate from old survival patterns?
- What positive feedback did I receive that I can choose to believe?
- How did I honor my values and needs today?
- What am I grateful for in my journey of growth?

Weekly Identity Check-in:

Every week, ask yourself:

- In what ways am I living more authentically than last week?
- What old patterns am I ready to release?
- What aspects of my true self do I want to express more often?
- How can I better align my actions with my values this week?

Remember, rewriting your narrative is not about denying your past or pretending your experiences didn't happen. It's about placing those experiences in a context that empowers rather than limits you. You are not defined by what happened to you; you are defined by how you choose to respond, heal, and grow. Your story is still being written, and you get to hold the pen.

Chapter 8: Low Contact, No Contact, and Everything In Between

One of the most difficult decisions you'll face when dealing with toxic family members is determining the level of contact that protects your well-being while honoring your emotional needs and circumstances. There's no one-size-fits-all solution to this dilemma, and what works for one person may not work for another. The key is understanding your options, honestly assessing your situation, and choosing the approach that best serves your healing and growth.

This chapter explores the various levels of contact you can choose to maintain with toxic family members, from complete no contact to modified low contact arrangements. We'll examine what each option looks like in practice, how to implement them effectively, and how to navigate the unique challenges and benefits of each approach. Most importantly, we'll help you determine what's healthiest for you at this point in your journey, while acknowledging that your needs may evolve over time.

Understanding Your Options

The spectrum of contact with toxic family members ranges from complete no contact to full engagement, with numerous variations in between. Understanding these options can help you make informed decisions about what might work best for your specific situation and healing needs.

No Contact means completely cutting off all communication and interaction with the toxic family member. This includes not responding to calls, texts, emails, or social media messages, not attending events where they'll be present, and having no indirect contact through other family members or mutual friends. No contact is often the most protective option for severe cases of abuse or when other approaches have repeatedly failed.

Low Contact involves maintaining minimal, highly structured interaction with the toxic family member. This might include brief phone calls on holidays, attending major family events with strict time limits, or responding to essential communications while ignoring non-essential contact. Low contact allows for some connection while maintaining protective boundaries.

Modified Contact includes various creative arrangements tailored to specific situations. This might involve contact only through a trusted intermediary, interaction only in public settings, communication only through text or email, or contact only for specific purposes like coordinating care for an elderly parent.

Structured Contact means maintaining regular but highly boundaried interaction. This might include scheduled phone calls with clear time limits, visits with predetermined end times, or communication that follows specific rules about acceptable topics and behavior.

The Gray Rock Method involves becoming as uninteresting and unresponsive as possible during necessary interactions. You provide minimal responses, share no personal information, and avoid engaging emotionally, making yourself a boring target for manipulation or drama.

Each approach has its advantages and challenges, and what works best for you may depend on factors like the severity of the toxicity, your support system, practical considerations like shared grandchildren or aging parents, your emotional resilience, and your personal values and goals.

No Contact: The Complete Break

No contact is often seen as the most extreme option, but for many people dealing with severe toxicity, it becomes the only viable choice for protecting their mental health and creating space for healing. No contact means exactly what it says—no communication or interaction of any kind with the toxic family member.

What No Contact Looks Like

No contact involves blocking phone numbers, email addresses, and social media accounts. It means not responding to any attempts at communication, no matter how urgent they may seem. It includes not attending family gatherings where the toxic person will be present, or attending only if you can be certain they won't be there. It also means asking other family members not to share information about you with the toxic person or to relay messages from them.

In practice, no contact might mean missing family weddings, funerals, or holiday celebrations. It might involve choosing not to visit a dying parent or grandparent. These decisions can be agonizing, but for some people, the alternative, exposing themselves to continued abuse or manipulation, is worse than missing these events.

No contact also extends to indirect forms of contact. This means not checking their social media profiles, not asking mutual friends or family members for updates about them, and not seeking information about their life or well-being. True no contact requires complete disconnection from their world, which can look like having no contact with anyone who has contact with the toxic person.

When No Contact Might Be Necessary

No contact is often the healthiest choice when:

- The family member has been physically, sexually, or severely emotionally abusive
- They refuse to acknowledge harmful behavior or take responsibility for their actions
- They consistently violate boundaries despite clear consequences
- Contact with them triggers severe anxiety, depression, or trauma responses
- They engage in stalking, harassment, or threatening behavior
- They attempt to sabotage your relationships, career, or well-being
- Previous attempts at low contact or structured contact have failed repeatedly
- Their presence in your life prevents you from healing and moving forward

Benefits of No Contact

No contact can provide complete protection from further harm and manipulation. It eliminates the emotional drain of managing a toxic relationship and creates space for healing without ongoing triggers. It allows you to focus entirely on your own growth and well-being without having to navigate the complex dynamics of maintaining any level of relationship with someone who has harmed you.

Many people report feeling a profound sense of relief and peace after implementing no contact. Without the constant stress of managing a toxic relationship, they find they have more energy for positive relationships and personal growth. They may sleep better, experience less anxiety, and find it easier to trust their own perceptions and feelings.

No contact also sends a clear message that you will not tolerate abusive behavior. While the toxic person may not receive or understand this message, it's important for your own sense of self-respect and empowerment.

Challenges of No Contact

No contact can be extremely difficult emotionally, especially in the beginning. You may experience intense guilt, doubt about your decision, or grief for the relationship you wished you could have had. Other family members may pressure you to reconcile or blame you for "breaking up the family."

Practical challenges can include missing important family events, having to make alternative arrangements for holidays and celebrations, and potentially losing relationships with other family members who don't support your decision. You may also face harassment or increased contact attempts initially, as the toxic person tries to regain control.

The finality of no contact can feel frightening, especially if you've never set such firm boundaries before. You might worry about missing opportunities for reconciliation or regret your decision if the person changes or dies while you're estranged.

Implementing No Contact

If you decide no contact is right for you, it's important to implement it clearly and consistently. Inform the person directly if possible, stating your decision clearly and briefly without extensive explanation or justification. Something like "I've decided I need to end contact between us. Please don't contact me in any way" is sufficient.

Block their phone number, email addresses, and social media profiles. Set up email filters to automatically delete messages from them. Consider changing your phone number if they continue attempting to contact you through different numbers.

Inform other family members and mutual friends about your decision and ask them not to share information about you or relay messages. Be clear that you don't want updates about the toxic person's life or guilt trips about your decision.

Document any harassment or attempts to contact you after you've requested no contact. This documentation may be important if you need to involve law enforcement or obtain a restraining order.

Prepare for potential escalation in the toxic person's behavior initially. They may increase their attempts to contact you, spread rumors about you, or try to turn other family members against you. Having a support system in place and a plan for handling these behaviors is crucial.

Low Contact: Minimal Interaction with Maximum Protection

Low contact is a middle-ground approach that allows for some level of connection while maintaining strong protective boundaries. This option works well for people who aren't ready for complete no contact but need significant protection from ongoing toxicity.

What Low Contact Looks Like

Low contact involves severely limiting both the frequency and depth of interactions with the toxic family member. You might have brief phone conversations only on major holidays, send birthday cards without personal messages, or attend large family gatherings where you can avoid one-on-one interaction.

Communication in low-contact arrangements is typically superficial and factual. You might discuss the weather, share basic life updates, or coordinate practical matters, but you avoid sharing personal feelings, seeking emotional support, or engaging in deeper conversations that could lead to manipulation or conflict.

Low contact often includes specific rules about acceptable topics of conversation and consequences for boundary violations. For example, you might end a phone call if the conversation turns to criticism or guilt-tripping, or leave an event if the toxic person begins engaging in inappropriate behavior.

Benefits of Low Contact

Low contact allows you to maintain some connection with the person while protecting yourself from the worst of their toxic behavior. It can be especially beneficial when other family members are involved—you might choose low contact with a toxic parent to maintain relationships with siblings or to ensure you can still see grandchildren.

This approach can reduce guilt compared to complete no contact, as you're still "making an effort" to maintain the relationship. It also allows for the possibility that the relationship might improve over time if the toxic person becomes willing to change their behavior.

Low contact can also be a stepping stone either toward healing the relationship if real change occurs, or toward no contact if the limited interaction proves that the toxicity continues unchanged.

Challenges of Low Contact

Low contact requires significant emotional energy to maintain. You must constantly monitor and manage your boundaries, which can be exhausting. The toxic person may interpret any contact as an invitation to push for more, leading to ongoing pressure and boundary testing.

The limited nature of low contact can be frustrating for both parties. The toxic person may feel rejected and increase their manipulative behavior, while you may find the superficial nature of the interactions unsatisfying or painful.

Low contact can also be confusing for other family members, who may not understand why you're willing to have some contact but not more. They may continue to pressure you to "work things out" or increase your level of engagement.

Implementing Low Contact Successfully

Successful low contact requires clear, consistent boundaries that you're willing to enforce. Decide in advance what types of contact you're willing to have and under what circumstances. Be specific about frequency (monthly phone calls, major holidays only), duration (fifteen-minute calls, one-hour visits), and acceptable topics.

Prepare standard responses for common manipulation tactics. Have phrases ready like "I'm not willing to discuss that," "I need to go now," or "That's not something I can help you with." Practice ending conversations or leaving situations when your boundaries are violated.

Control the terms of contact as much as possible. Initiate calls rather than answering theirs, choose public meeting places, set time limits for visits, and have your own transportation to events so you can leave when necessary.

Keep interactions focused on practical matters or neutral topics. Avoid sharing personal information about your relationships, work struggles, health issues, or other topics that could be used for manipulation or criticism.

Modified Contact Approaches

Sometimes, neither no contact nor traditional low contact feels right for your situation. Modified contact approaches involve creative solutions tailored to your specific circumstances and needs.

Contact Through Intermediaries

This approach involves maintaining a connection through a trusted third party who can filter communication and interactions. For example, you might communicate with a toxic parent only through a trusted sibling who can share essential information while protecting you from direct manipulation.

Intermediary contact can be particularly useful when coordinating care for aging parents, managing family business matters, or staying connected to extended family. The intermediary must be someone who understands the dynamics and is willing to maintain clear boundaries on your behalf.

Public-Only Interactions

Some people find they can tolerate limited interaction with toxic family members in public settings where the person is likely to be on their best behavior. This might involve attending large family gatherings but avoiding smaller, private interactions where inappropriate behavior is more likely.

Public-only interactions rely on the toxic person's concern about their public image to maintain appropriate behavior. However, this approach requires you to have strong boundaries and be prepared to leave if the person begins acting inappropriately despite the public setting.

Written Communication Only

Limiting contact to written communication (email or text) can provide protection from the emotional intensity of verbal interactions while creating a record of all communication. Written communication allows you to think carefully about your responses and avoid being caught off-guard by manipulation tactics.

This approach can be particularly effective for managing practical matters like coordinating family events or sharing necessary information. You can take time to craft measured responses and avoid the immediate emotional triggers of hearing their voice or tone.

Time-Limited Interactions

Some people find they can handle brief, structured interactions with toxic family members. This might involve fifteen-minute phone calls once a month, one-hour visits twice a year, or attending family events for a predetermined length of time.

Time-limited interactions require clear communication about the limits and consistent enforcement. You might say, "I can visit for two hours on Sunday afternoon," and then leave at the predetermined time regardless of pressure to stay longer.

The Gray Rock Method

The Gray Rock method is a specialized approach for managing necessary interactions with toxic family members when other forms of limited contact aren't possible. This technique involves making yourself as uninteresting and unengaging as possible during interactions.

How Gray Rock Works

When using the Gray Rock method, you provide minimal responses to questions, share no personal information, and avoid showing emotional reactions to provocative behavior. You become as boring and unrewarding as possible for the toxic person to interact with.

Gray Rock responses are brief, factual, and emotionally neutral. Instead of sharing news about your new job, you might say, "Work is fine." Instead of discussing relationship problems, you say, "Everything's okay." Instead of reacting to criticism or provocations, you respond with "Mmm" or "I see".

The goal is to provide no emotional supply for the toxic person while avoiding outright rudeness or obvious avoidance that might escalate conflict. You're present but unengaging, available but unrewarding to interact with.

When to Use Gray Rock

Gray Rock can be effective when you must maintain some contact due to practical circumstances like shared custody of children, family business obligations, or caregiving responsibilities. It's also useful for family events where complete avoidance isn't possible.

This method works particularly well with narcissistic family members who thrive on emotional reactions. By providing no emotional supply, positive or negative, you remove their incentive to engage in manipulative behavior.

Gray Rock can also be a temporary strategy while you prepare for lower contact or no contact arrangements. It can help you practice emotional detachment and reduce the intensity of interactions while you build the resources and support needed for firmer boundaries.

Challenges of Gray Rock

Gray Rock requires significant emotional self-control and can be emotionally exhausting to maintain. It may feel inauthentic or uncomfortable, especially if you're naturally expressive or empathetic. The toxic person may escalate their behavior initially in an attempt to provoke a reaction.

Other family members may not understand your behavior and may pressure you to be more engaging or responsive. They might interpret your Gray Rock approach as rude or cold, leading to additional family conflict.

Gray Rock also doesn't provide the same level of protection as lower contact approaches. You're still exposed to the toxic person's behavior, even if you're not engaging with it emotionally.

Choosing What's Right for You

Deciding on the right level of contact with toxic family members is deeply personal and depends on numerous factors unique to your situation. There's no universal "right" answer, and what works for someone else may not work for you.

Factors to Consider

Severity of toxicity: More severe abuse or manipulation typically requires stronger boundaries. Physical violence, threats, or severe emotional abuse often necessitate no contact for safety reasons.

Your emotional resilience: Honestly assess your current capacity to handle interactions with the toxic person. If you're early in your healing journey, you may need stricter boundaries than you might need later.

Support system: Having strong support from friends, chosen family, or mental health professionals can make lower levels of contact more manageable. Isolation makes any level of contact more risky.

Practical considerations: Shared children, aging parents needing care, family businesses, or financial entanglements may influence what levels of contact are practically possible.

Other family relationships: Consider how your decision might affect relationships with other family members you want to maintain. Sometimes, creative solutions can help you maintain these connections while protecting yourself.

Your values and beliefs: Some people feel that completely cutting off family members conflicts with their religious or cultural values. Others feel that maintaining any contact with an abuser violates their values around self-respect.

Past attempts: If you've tried low contact or structured contact repeatedly without success, it may be time to consider no contact. Conversely, if you've never tried setting boundaries, you might start with lower levels of contact.

Assessment Questions

Ask yourself these questions to help clarify what level of contact might be appropriate:

- How do I typically feel during and after interactions with this person?
- What specific behaviors or patterns am I trying to protect myself from?
- What, if any, are my goals for this relationship?
- What practical considerations do I need to account for?
- What level of contact feels manageable for me right now?
- What would I need to see change for me to feel comfortable with more contact?
- What support do I have in place to help me maintain my chosen boundaries?
- What are the potential consequences of different levels of contact, and which am I most comfortable accepting?

Starting Points and Evolution

Remember that your decision about contact levels doesn't have to be permanent. Many people find it helpful to start with stricter boundaries and gradually adjust based on their healing progress and the toxic person's behavior.

You might begin with no contact to create space for initial healing, then gradually introduce limited contact if and when you feel stronger and the other person demonstrates genuine change. Alternatively, you might start with low contact and move to no contact if the limited interaction proves too difficult or ineffective.

The key is to regularly reassess your situation and be willing to adjust your boundaries as needed. What serves you now may not serve you in six months or two years, and that's perfectly acceptable.

Preparing for Different Outcomes

Whatever level of contact you choose, it's important to prepare for various possible outcomes and have plans in place for managing challenges that may arise.

Preparing for Escalation

Many toxic family members escalate their behavior when new boundaries are implemented. They may increase their contact attempts, engage in guilt-tripping or manipulation, recruit other family members to pressure you, or even engage in more serious harassment or stalking behavior.

Prepare for this possibility by:

- Building your support network before implementing boundaries
- Documenting any harassment or inappropriate behavior
- Having a safety plan if there's any possibility of physical danger
- Preparing responses to common manipulation tactics
- Considering involving law enforcement if harassment occurs

Managing Family Backlash

Other family members may not understand or support your decision to limit contact with a toxic relative. They may pressure you to reconcile, blame you for family problems, or even cut off their relationships with you.

Prepare for this by:

- Having clear explanations ready for those who need them
- Identifying which family members are likely to be supportive
- Building connections with chosen family who understand your situation
- Preparing emotionally for possible losses of other relationships
- Remembering that your healing is worth a temporary family disruption

Handling Special Occasions

Holidays, birthdays, weddings, funerals, and other special occasions can be particularly challenging when you've limited contact with a toxic family member. These events often involve family pressure, emotional triggers, and difficult decisions about attendance.

Prepare by:

- Deciding in advance which events you'll attend and under what conditions
- Creating alternative celebrations with chosen family
- Having exit strategies for events you do attend
- Preparing responses to questions about the absent person
- Building new traditions that don't include the toxic family member

Creating Your Contact Plan

Once you've decided on your approach, create a specific plan that outlines your boundaries and how you'll maintain them.

Writing Your Boundaries

Document your decision in writing, including:

- The level of contact you're choosing and why
- Specific rules about frequency, duration, and types of interaction
- Consequences for boundary violations
- How you'll handle special occasions and family events
- Who you'll ask for support and how
- Signs that you might need to adjust your boundaries

Communicating Your Decision

Decide who needs to know about your decision and how you'll communicate it:

- Will you inform the toxic person directly, or simply implement the boundaries?
- Which other family members need to know, and what will you tell them?
- How will you handle questions or pressure from others?
- What support do you need in communicating your decision?

Monitoring and Adjusting

Plan to regularly review your boundaries:

- How often will you assess whether your current approach is working?

- What signs will indicate you need to adjust your boundaries?
- Who can help you objectively evaluate your situation?
- How will you make changes if needed?

Reflection: Choosing What's Healthiest for You Now

Use these exercises to help you determine what level of contact feels right for your situation and to create a sustainable plan for maintaining your chosen boundaries.

Current Situation Assessment

Relationship Impact Inventory:

For the toxic family member you're considering limiting contact with, rate each area from 1 (no impact) to 5 (severe negative impact):

- My emotional well-being during interactions: ___
- My emotional well-being after interactions: ___
- My sleep patterns: ___
- My other relationships: ___
- My work or school performance: ___
- My physical health: ___
- My self-esteem: ___
- My ability to trust my own perceptions: ___
- My overall life satisfaction: ___

Total score: ___

Higher scores suggest you need stronger boundaries for your well-being.

Values and Priorities Exercise

Rank these priorities from most important (1) to least important (10) for you:

___ My mental health and well-being

___ Maintaining family traditions

___ Other family members' comfort with my decisions

___ My spiritual or religious beliefs about family

___ My children's relationships with extended family

___ My partner's comfort with family dynamics

____ Financial security or inheritance considerations

____ My reputation in the community

____ Avoiding conflict at family events

____ My personal growth and healing

Reflection:

How do your top priorities align with different contact options? What level of contact best honors your most important values?

Contact Options Exploration

For each level of contact, complete this assessment:

No Contact:

- Potential benefits for me: _____
- Potential challenges for me: _____
- Impact on other relationships: _____
- Practical considerations: _____
- My comfort level (1-10): ____

Low Contact:

- Potential benefits for me: _____
- Potential challenges for me: _____
- Impact on other relationships: _____
- Practical considerations: _____
- My comfort level (1-10): ____

Modified Contact (specify type):

- Potential benefits for me: _____
- Potential challenges for me: _____
- Impact on other relationships: _____
- Practical considerations: _____
- My comfort level (1-10): ____

Boundary Setting Worksheet

My chosen approach: _____

Specific boundaries I will set:

- Frequency of contact: _____
- Duration of interactions: _____
- Types of acceptable communication: _____
- Topics I won't discuss: _____
- Events I will/won't attend: _____
- Total time I will attend events: _____
- Consequences for boundary violations: _____

My support system:

- People who support my decision: _____
- Professional support I have access to: _____
- Resources I can use when struggling: _____

Signs I need to reassess my boundaries:

- If I consistently feel _____ after contact
- If the person _____
- If my _____ is significantly impacted
- If I find myself _____

Implementation Timeline

Immediate steps (next week):

- Finalize my contact decision
- Prepare any necessary communications
- Alert my support system
- Block numbers/social media if needed
- Other: _____

Short-term steps (next month):

- Implement boundaries consistently
- Handle initial reactions/escalation
- Adjust practical arrangements as needed
- Other: _____

Long-term maintenance (ongoing):

- Regular boundary assessment
- Continued work with the support system
- Adjustments as my needs change
- Other: _____

Emergency Plan

If the toxic person escalates their behavior:

- I will _____
- I will contact _____
- I will go to _____ for safety
- I will document _____

If other family members pressure me:

- I will remind myself that _____
- I will respond by saying _____
- I will seek support from _____
- I will limit contact with pressuring family members by _____

If I start to doubt my decision:

- I will reread _____
- I will remind myself that _____
- I will talk to _____
- I will review my boundary assessment and _____

Affirmations for Contact Decisions

Choose affirmations that resonate with your chosen approach:

For No Contact:

- "I deserve complete protection from abuse and manipulation"
- "My healing is more important than others' comfort with my boundaries"
- "I am not responsible for maintaining toxic relationships"
- "Complete separation allows me to create the life I deserve"

For Low Contact:

- "I can maintain minimal contact while protecting my well-being"
- "I have the right to determine the terms of my relationships"
- "Limited contact is still contact, and I am not abandoning anyone"
- "I can be civil without being emotionally available"

For Modified Contact:

- "Creative solutions can honor both my needs and my circumstances"
- "I can find ways to stay connected while staying protected"
- "My unique situation requires a unique approach, and that's okay"
- "I trust myself to know what works for me"

Remember, there is no perfect solution when dealing with toxic family members. The goal is not to find the "right" answer but to find the approach that best protects your well-being while honoring your values and circumstances. Your choice may evolve as you heal and grow, and that's not only acceptable—it's healthy. Trust yourself to know what you need right now, while remaining open to adjusting your boundaries as your needs change over time.

Chapter 9: When the Abuser Is Dying or Sick

Perhaps no situation tests your boundaries and resolves more intensely than learning that a toxic family member is seriously ill or dying. The combination of societal pressure, guilt, hope for deathbed reconciliation, and your own complex emotions can create an overwhelming storm of confusion and self-doubt. This chapter addresses one of the most challenging scenarios you may face in your healing journey: how to navigate your own needs and boundaries when confronted with the mortality of someone who has caused you significant harm.

Society has deeply ingrained expectations about how we should respond when family members are dying. We're told that death changes everything, that we should forgive and forget, that we'll regret it forever if we don't reconcile before it's too late. These messages can be particularly intense when coming from well-meaning friends, religious communities, or other family members who don't understand the full extent of the abuse you've experienced.

This chapter will help you navigate the complex emotions, external pressures, and difficult decisions that arise when an abuser is facing death or serious illness. We'll explore how to manage guilt and external pressure, examine what it means to choose not to show up, and discuss how to grieve and honor your healing journey even in the face of death. Most importantly, we'll help you give yourself permission to choose what's healthiest for you, regardless of what others expect or demand.

The Myth of Deathbed Reconciliation

One of the most pervasive and harmful myths surrounding death and family relationships is the idea that impending death automatically creates the conditions for meaningful reconciliation. Movies, television shows, and cultural narratives consistently portray deathbed scenes where years of hurt and abuse are magically resolved through tearful forgiveness and expressions of love. These portrayals, while emotionally satisfying in fiction, can create unrealistic expectations and additional pressure for real families dealing with complex trauma histories.

The reality is that death doesn't fundamentally change a person's character or their capacity for genuine remorse and accountability. Long-term family estrangements usually happen for very good reasons: physical, emotional, and/or sexual abuse, untreated addiction, untended mental illness, a family member's inability to come to terms with another's sexual or gender identity, or because the dynamic between family members is just too painful to bear. A narcissistic, manipulative, or abusive family member doesn't typically become self-aware and genuinely apologetic simply because they're facing mortality. In fact, the fear and vulnerability that often accompany serious illness can sometimes intensify existing negative patterns rather than resolve them.

Many toxic individuals become more demanding, manipulative, or controlling when they're ill, using their condition as leverage to regain access to family members who have established boundaries. They may make promises of change that they have no intention of keeping, or offer superficial apologies that lack genuine understanding or accountability. The urgency created by their condition can pressure family members into accepting these hollow gestures as meaningful reconciliation.

Furthermore, true reconciliation requires several elements that are often absent in relationships with toxic family members: genuine acknowledgment of wrongdoing, authentic remorse, understanding of the impact of their behavior, and a commitment to different behavior going forward. When someone is dying, the opportunity for sustained behavioral change is obviously limited, making genuine reconciliation practically impossible even if the other elements were present.

It's also important to recognize that the desire for deathbed reconciliation often comes more from the needs of the surviving family members than from any genuine change in the dying person. Adult children may desperately want their parents to finally see and acknowledge them, to express love and pride, or to take responsibility for past harm. This longing is natural and understandable, but acting on it can lead to further disappointment and trauma if the toxic person is incapable of providing what's needed.

The pressure to reconcile before death can also come from a fear of regret—the worry that you'll feel guilty or remorseful forever if you don't make peace before it's too late. However, in my experience of serving people in hospice, you are equally as likely to regret what you do in haste as what you don't do out of caution. Enormous harm can be done, both to the dying person and their family, if they reconnect out of a panicked fear of regret. A visit that reopens old wounds can bring more regret than no visit at all.

Understanding Your Complex Emotions

Learning that an abusive family member is seriously ill or dying typically triggers a complex mix of emotions that can feel overwhelming and contradictory. You might experience relief that the person can no longer hurt you, guilt about feeling relieved, sadness for the relationship that never was, anger about missed opportunities for genuine healing, fear about family pressure to reconcile, and confusion about what you "should" feel or do.

These mixed emotions are completely normal and don't indicate confusion, lack of healing, or moral failure on your part. They reflect the complicated nature of relationships with people who have both loved and harmed us, or who we wished could have loved us in healthy ways. Grieving someone you never truly loved—or who could never love you in healthy ways—doesn't mean you're confused. It simply reflects the complexity of loss.

The complexity of grief is difficult to describe or understand, especially when it's a family member one has been estranged from. We have every right to feel sad, angry, resentful, or even guilty, whether the estrangement was our choice or not. It's possible to simultaneously feel glad that someone can no longer hurt you while also feeling sad that they're suffering, or to feel grief for their impending death while also feeling relieved about the end of a difficult relationship.

You might find yourself hoping against hope that the person will finally acknowledge the harm they've caused, take responsibility for their behavior, and express genuine love and remorse. This hope is natural, especially if you've spent years longing for their validation and acceptance. However, it's important to protect yourself from being manipulated by these hopes or pressured into situations that could cause additional trauma.

Some survivors experience a resurgence of traumatic memories when learning about an abuser's illness or impending death. The stress of the situation, combined with family pressure and your own complex emotions, can trigger responses similar to those you experienced during the original abuse. If this happens to you, it's a sign that you need extra support and self-care during this difficult time.

You might feel angry that the person gets to die without ever being held accountable for their behavior, or frustrated that their death will be mourned by people who didn't experience their abuse. These feelings of injustice are valid and common among survivors.

It's also normal to feel pressure to be the "bigger person" or to worry about how your response will be perceived by others. Family members, friends, or community members might expect you to put aside past hurts in the face of death, not understanding that doing so could be harmful to your healing and well-being. Your primary obligation is to yourself and your own mental health, not to meeting others' expectations about how you should respond to the situation.

Managing External Pressure and Guilt

When an abusive family member is dying, the external pressure to reconcile or "do the right thing" can be intense and relentless. This pressure typically comes from several sources and can feel overwhelming when combined with your own complex emotions about the situation.

Family members who haven't experienced the abuse directly, or who have normalized it over the years, may genuinely believe that death changes everything and that reconciliation is both possible and necessary. There are the insensitive and unaware questions or comments, such as "But they're your family; you should have talked to them", or guilt trips such as "Why are you sad? You didn't talk to them anyway." These family members may have their own reasons for wanting family unity, including their own discomfort with family conflict or their need to maintain their own relationships with the dying person.

Religious or spiritual communities can also be sources of significant pressure, often emphasizing concepts like forgiveness, honoring parents, or Christian charity without understanding the full context of abuse and trauma. Well-meaning clergy or community members might quote scriptures about forgiveness or tell you that reconciliation is necessary for your own spiritual well-being, not recognizing that forced reconciliation can actually be harmful to survivors.

Healthcare providers, social workers, or other professionals involved in the dying person's care might also inadvertently pressure you to visit or reconcile, especially if they don't understand the history of abuse. They may frame your absence as abandonment or suggest that the dying person needs all their family around them, not recognizing that your presence might not be wanted by the dying person or be healthy for you.

The dying person themselves might engage in manipulation tactics designed to pressure you into contact. They might send messages through other family members about how much they want to see you, how sorry they are, or how little time they have left. They might make promises about changed behavior, inheritance, or other inducements designed to get you to visit. It's important to remember that these tactics are often consistent with their historical patterns of manipulation and may not represent genuine change or remorse.

Managing this external pressure requires clear boundaries and strong support systems. It can be helpful to prepare standard responses for common pressures: "I appreciate your concern, but I've made the decision that's healthiest for me," "This is a private family matter that I'm handling in my own way," or "I understand you mean well, but I need you to respect my boundaries about this situation."

You do not owe anyone an explanation for these feelings, nor do you need permission to feel them. While it might be helpful to share your reasoning with trusted, supportive people, you don't need to justify your decision to anyone who is pressuring you to act against your own best interests.

Choosing Not to Show Up

Despite intense external pressure and your own complex emotions, there are many valid reasons why choosing not to visit or reconcile with a dying abusive family member might be the healthiest decision for you. This choice doesn't make you heartless, cruel, or unforgiving—it makes you someone who prioritizes their own well-being and recognizes the importance of maintaining boundaries even in difficult circumstances.

Valid Reasons for Staying Away

Protecting your mental health: If visiting would trigger severe anxiety, depression, PTSD symptoms, or other mental health crises, staying away is an act of self-care rather than cruelty. Your mental health is as important as anyone else's physical health, and you have the right to protect it.

Preventing re-traumatization: If the dying person is likely to use the visit as an opportunity to continue abusive behavior, blame you for family problems, or engage in other harmful actions, staying away protects you from additional trauma. Death doesn't automatically stop abusive behavior.

Avoiding manipulation: If you believe the person is using their illness or impending death to manipulate you back into an abusive relationship or to gain access they previously didn't have, maintaining your boundaries is appropriate. Genuine remorse doesn't come with manipulation tactics.

Protecting your family: If you have children, a spouse, or other family members who would be negatively affected by your involvement with the dying person, protecting them is more important than satisfying others' expectations about deathbed reconciliation.

Honoring your authentic feelings: If you feel relief, indifference, or even happiness about the person's impending death, trying to fake grief or love during a visit would be inauthentic and potentially harmful to your emotional well-being. It's okay to feel your grief. It's also okay not to feel anything at all. These feelings can also coexist.

Maintaining consistency with your values: If reconciling would violate your personal values about self-respect, enabling abusive behavior, or teaching your children about healthy boundaries, staying true to these values is more important than appearing socially acceptable.

Preventing false hope: If you know that any contact would create false hope for an ongoing relationship that you're not willing or able to provide, it might be kinder to both of you to maintain distance.

What Staying Away Looks Like

Choosing not to visit a dying abusive family member might mean not going to the hospital or hospice facility, not attending bedside vigils, not participating in family meetings about their care, and not being present at the moment of death. It might also mean not attending funeral services, memorial services, or other events surrounding their death.

This choice might require making alternative arrangements for things you do want to participate in. For example, you might choose to attend the funeral but not the bedside vigil, or to visit the gravesite privately after the burial rather than attending the service. You might write a letter to express your thoughts and feelings without delivering it in person, or make a donation to a meaningful cause rather than sending flowers to the funeral.

Don't insist that anyone contact an estranged family member before they die, or that they will regret it if they don't. Remember that if you yourself are trying to decide whether to reconnect with an estranged, dying family member, don't let yourself be bullied. The decision is yours, and yours alone.

Staying away also means being prepared for the reactions of others. Some family members might be angry, disappointed, or confused by your choice. They might make accusations about your character, threaten consequences, or try to guilt you into changing your mind. Preparing for these reactions and having support systems in place is crucial for maintaining your boundaries during this difficult time.

The Aftermath of Staying Away

After the person dies, you might experience a complex mix of emotions about your decision to stay away. You might feel relief that you maintained your boundaries, sadness about the final end of any possibility for the relationship you wanted, guilt about not being there, or vindication if the person continued to behave badly until the end.

Most felt no obligation to go to the funeral or to support others in the family, no matter how long they had been cut off or who had ended the relationship. Those who did not go said they had no regrets. Some expected to be criticized or judged for not attending, but they said that would not affect their decision.

It's important to remember that your decision was made based on the information and emotional resources you had at the time, and with your well-being as the priority. Even if you experience some regret or sadness about staying away, this doesn't mean you made the wrong decision. Complex situations often result in complex feelings, and it's possible to feel sad about your choice while still knowing it was the right one for your circumstances.

The Reality of Deathbed Visits

For those who do choose to visit a dying abusive family member, it's important to have realistic expectations about what these visits might look like. The fantasy of meaningful reconciliation, heartfelt apologies, and peaceful closure is often far from the reality of these encounters.

Many survivors who do visit report that the dying person was still manipulative, self-centered, or abusive during their final interactions. Some dying people use these visits as opportunities to continue old patterns of blame, guilt-tripping, or emotional manipulation. Others may be medicated, confused, or unable to engage in meaningful conversation. Still others might make superficial apologies or promises that lack genuine understanding or accountability.

Even when the dying person does express remorse, it may not provide the healing or closure you're hoping for. Decades of hurt and trauma can't be undone by a single conversation, and you might leave feeling more frustrated or disappointed. The gap between what you need for healing and what the person is able to provide may remain as wide as ever.

Some visitors report feeling like they're performing a role during these visits—playing the part of the loving, forgiving family member while feeling disconnected from their authentic emotions. This performance can be exhausting and emotionally damaging, especially if you feel pressured to maintain it for extended periods.

Reaching out to an estranged family member as they near the end of life is a deeply personal decision, and it may not always bring the comfort or closure you imagine. Sometimes the urge to act quickly can lead to choices made in haste, which may carry their own regrets. At the same time, choosing not to reach out—often out of caution or self-protection—can leave you questioning what might have been. There is no perfect path in these moments, only the one that best honors both your boundaries and your well-being. Whatever choice you make, it is valid because it reflects the truth of your circumstances and the care you are offering yourself.

If you do choose to visit, it's important to prepare yourself mentally and emotionally. Set clear boundaries about what you will and won't discuss, how long you'll stay, and what behavior you'll tolerate. Have an exit strategy in place and be prepared to use it if the interaction becomes harmful. Bring a supportive person with you if possible, and plan for self-care activities after the visit.

Grieving Without Reconciliation

One of the most challenging aspects of dealing with an abusive family member's death is learning to grieve without the reconciliation that society tells us is necessary for "proper" mourning. You have the right to grieve in your own way, for your own reasons, and according to your own timeline, regardless of whether you reconciled before the person's death.

Your grief might not look like traditional mourning. It may seem there is no grieving for someone you hardly knew, but it is the loss of what could have been, not what was. You might feel relief mixed with sadness, anger mixed with love, or a complex combination of emotions that don't fit into neat categories. You might grieve for the person you wished they could have been, for the relationship you never had, or for the childhood you lost to their dysfunction. All of these forms of grief are valid and normal.

Grief for an estranged parent is very complicated. As I said, you have a lot of feelings and nowhere in particular to direct them. It is almost as if you don't deserve to grieve. You might also feel guilty about not feeling "sad enough" or worried that your lack of traditional grief symptoms means you're heartless or unnatural. It's important to understand that there's no "right" way to grieve, especially when the relationship was complicated by abuse and trauma.

Some survivors find it helpful to create their own private rituals for processing the person's death. This might involve writing a letter you never send, creating artwork that expresses your feelings, planting something in memory of what could have been, or simply taking time for reflection and self-care. Use ritual: if you can't go to the funeral, or there is not one, plan your own memorial service. These personal rituals can be more meaningful than traditional funeral services that may not reflect your actual relationship with the person.

There is no timeline for anyone to heal. It's also important to allow for the possibility that your feelings about the person's death may change over time. You might initially feel relief that transforms into sadness, or sadness that evolves into acceptance. Grief is not a linear process, and this is especially true when the relationship was complicated by abuse and trauma.

Supporting Others While Protecting Yourself

The death of a family member affects the entire family system, and you might find yourself in the position of wanting to support other family members who are grieving while still protecting your own emotional well-being. This balancing act can be particularly challenging when the other family members don't understand or support your boundaries.

You might want to support siblings who are grieving, even if they don't understand your decision to stay away from the dying person. You might want to be there for your children as they process the death of a grandparent, even if that grandparent was abusive to you. You might want to help with practical arrangements for the funeral or memorial service without attending the events themselves.

It's possible to provide support while maintaining your boundaries, but it requires clear communication and careful planning. You might offer to help with specific tasks that don't require you to compromise your boundaries, such as coordinating meal deliveries, managing communications with extended family, or helping with practical arrangements from a distance.

You might also provide emotional support to other family members through individual conversations rather than group gatherings where the dying person might be discussed in ways that are difficult for you to hear. You can listen to their grief and offer comfort without having to participate in idealized memories or forgiveness narratives that don't reflect your experience.

However, it's important to recognize that you can't support everyone in the way they might want while also protecting your own well-being. Some family members might want you to provide support by abandoning your boundaries, attending events that would be harmful to you, or participating in narratives about the person that don't reflect your truth. In these cases, you might need to limit your support or provide it in ways that don't compromise your own healing.

The Aftermath: Death and Its Consequences

After an abusive family member dies, you might face a new set of challenges related to how their death is remembered and discussed by others. Family members who didn't experience the abuse might want to focus only on positive memories, leaving you feeling silenced about your own experiences. Community members might praise the person's character in ways that feel invalidating to survivors of their abuse.

You might feel pressure to participate in memorial activities that don't reflect your experience of the person, or to contribute to narratives about their life that minimize or ignore the harm they caused. It's important to remember that you have the right to your own truth about the person, regardless of how others choose to remember them.

Families often expect relatives to mourn any and every relative, even if the deceased was an abuser. Some survivors find it helpful to create their own ways of processing the person's death and their complicated relationship with them. This might involve writing your own honest account of the relationship, sharing your story with trusted friends or a therapist, or finding other survivors of the person's behavior to share experiences with.

You might also find that the person's death creates unexpected changes in family dynamics. Some family members might become more accepting of your boundaries and experiences, while others might become more critical or distant. The family system that was organized around the toxic person's needs and behaviors will need to reorganize, which can create both opportunities and challenges.

Trying to imagine the complexity of the death of an estranged parent is as futile as trying to imagine that we can recover from that death. Yet, we do heal, and it is the gradual realization that we will survive the loss that makes parental death so transforming. It's important to prepare for the possibility that the person's death won't bring the peace or closure you might hope for. While some survivors do experience relief or a sense of freedom after an abuser dies, others find that the complex feelings and family dynamics continue long after the person is gone.

Giving Yourself Permission

Perhaps the most important thing to remember when dealing with a dying abusive family member is that you have the right to make decisions based on what's healthiest for you, regardless of external pressure or social expectations. You don't need anyone's permission to maintain your boundaries, and you don't owe anyone access to you, even when they're dying.

For those still waiting for an external confirmation of their pain, the hardest but most liberating realization is this: You don't need their permission to tell your story. You don't need their validation to know it was real. You don't need a courtroom to reclaim your truth.

This permission includes the right to feel whatever you feel without judgment, to grieve in your own way and in your own time, to participate or not participate in end-of-life events according to your own comfort level, and to remember the person honestly rather than through rose-colored glasses.

You are not alone. Estrangements are extremely common, and everybody eventually dies. Because of the stigma surrounding both estrangement and death, it may not seem this way. Though you may feel alone right now, your experience is normal.

Giving yourself this permission often requires actively challenging the voices, both external and internal, that tell you what you "should" do in this situation. It means trusting your own judgment about what's best for your mental health and well-being, even when others disagree with your choices.

What I wish people knew is the unimaginable courage it takes to put yourself first. It's one of the highest acts of love that we can do for ourselves, and yet it's not always honored or respected. Your decision to prioritize your healing and well-being, even in the face of death, is not selfish. It's an act of self-preservation and self-respect that honors the hard work you've done to heal from abuse and trauma.

Reflection: Writing Your "Permission to Choose" Letter

Use this exercise to clarify your thoughts, feelings, and boundaries around a dying or seriously ill abusive family member. This letter is for you alone and can help you process your emotions and affirm your right to make choices that prioritize your well-being.

Your Personal Permission Letter

Write a letter to yourself giving yourself permission to handle this situation in whatever way feels healthiest for you. Consider including:

Permission to Feel:

"I give myself permission to feel whatever emotions arise about [person's name]'s illness/death, including..."

Permission to Choose:

"I give myself permission to choose the level of involvement that feels right for me, which might include..."

Permission to Change Your Mind:

"I give myself permission to change my decisions as my needs change, and I don't have to explain these changes to anyone who..."

Permission to Grieve Differently:

"I give myself permission to grieve in my own way, which might look different from others' expectations because..."

Permission to Protect Yourself:

"I give myself permission to prioritize my mental health and well-being over others' expectations by..."

Permission to Be Authentic:

"I give myself permission to be honest about my relationship with this person, rather than pretending..."

Addressing Your Fears and Doubts

Complete these statements:

"My biggest fear about my chosen response to this situation is..."

"I worry that others will think because..."

"I sometimes doubt my decision because..."

"What I need to remember when these doubts arise is..."

"The people who truly support me will..."

Clarifying Your Values and Boundaries

Reflect on these questions:

- What values are most important to me in this situation?
- How do my chosen actions align with these values?
- What boundaries do I need to maintain to protect my well-being?
- What would I tell a friend in a similar situation?
- What would I want my children (if applicable) to learn from how I handle this?

Creating Your Support Plan

Identify your support system:

- Who understands and supports my decision?
- Who can I talk to when I'm struggling with doubt or pressure?
- What professional support do I have available?
- What activities help me manage stress and maintain emotional balance?

Plan for challenging moments:

- How will I respond to guilt trips or pressure from family members?
- What will I do if I start to doubt my decision?
- How will I handle unexpected emotions that arise?
- What self-care practices will I prioritize during this time?

Affirmations for Your Journey

Choose affirmations that resonate with your situation:

- "I have the right to protect my mental health and well-being"
- "My healing journey is more important than others' comfort with my choices"
- "I can love someone from a distance while protecting myself from their toxicity"
- "Death doesn't erase abuse or automatically create obligation"
- "I trust my own judgment about what's best for me"
- "I don't need anyone's permission to prioritize my well-being"
- "My response to this situation reflects my strength, not my weakness"
- "I am not responsible for other people's emotions about my choices"

Letter to Your Future Self

Write a brief letter to yourself to read in the future, after this situation has passed:

"Dear Future Me,

As I write this, [person's name] is [dying/seriously ill], and I have chosen [your decision]. I want you to remember that this decision was made with love - love for myself, for my healing, and for the life I'm building.

If you're reading this and having any regrets or doubts, please remember:

[Include reminders of your reasons, your values, and the care you put into making this decision]

I hope you can look back on this time with compassion for the difficult position I was in and pride in the courage it took to honor my own needs.

With love and respect for our journey,

[Your name today]"

Emergency Reminders

Create a list of reminders to refer to when you're feeling pressured or doubtful.

- "I made this decision thoughtfully and with my well-being as the priority"
- "Other people's discomfort with my boundaries doesn't make them wrong"
- "I cannot heal a lifetime of damage with one deathbed visit"
- "Protecting myself from further harm is not cruel, it's necessary"
- "I deserve to feel safe and peaceful, even during family crises"

Remember, there is no "right" way to handle the death or serious illness of an abusive family member. Whatever choice you make—whether it's no contact, limited contact, or full engagement- the most important thing is that it serves your healing and well-being. Trust yourself to know what you need, and give yourself permission to choose accordingly. Your healing journey is valid and important, regardless of how others respond to your choices.

Chapter 10: Holidays, Birthdays, and the Pressure to Reconnect

Few situations test your resolve to maintain boundaries with toxic family members quite like holidays and special occasions. These events arrive with a potent mixture of cultural expectations, emotional triggers, and intense family pressure that can make even the strongest boundaries feel shaky. Whether it's Christmas morning, your birthday, Mother's Day, or a family wedding, these occasions carry deep emotional significance and societal scripts about how families "should" celebrate together.

The pressure during these times isn't just external; it often comes from within yourself. You might find yourself questioning your boundaries, wondering if you're being too harsh, or feeling guilty about missing family traditions. The romantic imagery of holidays and celebrations can trigger longing for the family you wish you had, making it harder to remember why you established boundaries in the first place.

This chapter will help you navigate these emotionally charged occasions while maintaining your well-being and honoring your healing journey. We'll explore why holidays are particularly challenging, how to manage the intense emotions they bring up, and practical strategies for creating new traditions that nourish rather than drain you. Most importantly, we'll help you develop a sustainable approach to special occasions that protects your progress while allowing you to celebrate in ways that feel authentic and joyful.

Why Holidays Are Emotional Landmines

Holidays and special occasions carry an emotional weight that goes far beyond their actual significance. They're loaded with childhood memories, cultural expectations, and deeply ingrained beliefs about what families are supposed to look and feel like. For those who grew up in toxic family systems, these occasions often represent both the best and worst memories—brief moments of connection alongside episodes of conflict, disappointment, and harm.

The Fantasy of Family Unity

Society bombards us with images of perfect family gatherings: everyone smiling around the dinner table, exchanging thoughtful gifts, sharing warm embraces, and creating magical memories together. These idealized portrayals set an impossible standard that even healthy families struggle to meet, but they're particularly painful for those from dysfunctional backgrounds.

When you've established boundaries with toxic family members, these cultural messages can feel like accusations. Every advertisement showing three generations laughing together, every movie depicting holiday reconciliation, every social media post about grateful families can trigger guilt and self-doubt about your choices.

The gap between the fantasy and your reality can be particularly stark during holidays. While others seem to be gathering with loving families, you might be spending the day alone or explaining to friends why you won't be joining family celebrations. This contrast can make you feel like an outsider, as if you've failed at one of life's most basic relationships.

Childhood Associations and Triggers

Holidays often trigger powerful memories from childhood, both positive and negative. You might remember the excitement of Christmas morning alongside the anxiety of wondering whether this would be the year your parents fought, drank too much, or disappointed you again. Birthday memories might include feeling ignored or having your special day overshadowed by family drama.

These mixed associations can create a complex emotional response to holidays. Part of you might long for the joy and magic you glimpsed in better moments, while another part remembers the pain and chaos that often accompanied these occasions. This internal conflict can make it difficult to enjoy holidays, even when you're in a safer environment.

The sensory triggers associated with holidays can also bring up unexpected emotional responses. The smell of a particular dish might transport you back to a traumatic family dinner, or hearing a favorite holiday song might remind you of times when you felt alone despite being surrounded by family.

The Pressure of "Should"

Holidays come with an enormous weight of "shoulds" that can feel overwhelming when you're trying to maintain boundaries with toxic family members. You "should" call your mother on Mother's Day. You "should" be grateful for your family. You "should" put differences aside for the holidays. You "should" think about what your grandmother would have wanted. You "should" give your family another chance.

These societal expectations are reinforced by religious teachings, cultural traditions, and well-meaning friends who don't understand the complexity of your family situation. They create a constant background pressure that can make you question your boundaries and feel guilty for prioritizing your well-being.

The "should" messages are particularly intense because they often come disguised as moral imperatives. Choosing to protect yourself from toxic family members during holidays can feel like violating fundamental values about love, forgiveness, and family loyalty, even when you intellectually know that your boundaries are necessary and healthy.

Anniversary Reactions and Trauma Triggers

For many people from toxic families, holidays are associated with some of their worst traumatic experiences. Family gatherings provided opportunities for abuse, neglect, or severe emotional harm because everyone was expected to be together and put on a happy face for the occasion.

These anniversary reactions can be intense and unpredictable. You might find yourself feeling anxious, depressed, or emotionally dysregulated as a holiday approaches, even if you're not consciously thinking about past trauma. Your body remembers the patterns and prepares for danger, even when you're now safe.

The forced intimacy and emotional intensity of holiday gatherings can also mirror the dynamics that made your family toxic in the first place. The pressure to perform happiness, the expectation of physical affection, the requirement to suppress conflict for the sake of the occasion—all of these can trigger trauma responses and make holidays feel unsafe.

Understanding the Pressure to Reconnect

The pressure to reconnect with toxic family members during holidays comes from multiple sources and can feel almost irresistible. Understanding where this pressure comes from can help you recognize it as an external influence rather than your own authentic desire for reconnection.

Cultural and Religious Messages

Most cultures and religions have strong teachings about the importance of family unity, especially during significant occasions. These messages often emphasize forgiveness, reconciliation, and putting aside differences for the sake of celebration. While these teachings may have positive intentions, they can create enormous pressure for those dealing with genuinely toxic family dynamics.

Religious messages about honoring parents, forgiving enemies, and maintaining family bonds can be particularly challenging. Well-meaning clergy or religious community members might encourage you to reach out to estranged family members during holy seasons, not understanding that doing so could be harmful to your mental health and spiritual well-being.

Cultural expectations around specific holidays can also create pressure. The expectation that everyone gathers for Christmas, that mothers are celebrated on Mother's Day, or that families come together for important birthdays can make your absence feel like a glaring violation of social norms.

Social Media and Comparison

Social media intensifies holiday pressure by providing a constant stream of seemingly perfect family celebrations. Everyone appears to be surrounded by loving relatives, sharing joyful moments, and creating beautiful memories together. These curated glimpses into others' lives can make your own situation feel abnormal or tragic by comparison.

It's important to remember that social media presents a highly edited version of reality. The families posting happy photos may have their own struggles, conflicts, and complications that aren't visible in their posts. The perfect dinner table photo doesn't show the fight that happened beforehand or the tension that existed underneath the smiles.

However, knowing this intellectually doesn't always protect you from the emotional impact of seeing others celebrate with intact families when you're dealing with estrangement or limited contact. The longing for what appears to be a "normal" family connection can be particularly acute during holiday seasons.

Well-Meaning Friends and Extended Family

Friends, extended family members, and acquaintances often pressure reconnection during holidays, believing they're being helpful or encouraging. They might suggest that holidays are the perfect time to "let bygones be bygones," remind you that "life is short," or express concern that you're missing precious time with family.

These suggestions usually come from people who haven't experienced severe family toxicity themselves. They may have had their own family conflicts and worked through them, leading them to believe that all family problems can be resolved with enough goodwill and effort. They don't understand that some family dynamics are genuinely harmful and that reconciliation isn't always possible or advisable.

Extended family members might also pressure reconnection because your boundaries affect their own family gatherings and relationships. They may feel caught in the middle or worry that acknowledging the validity of your boundaries would require them to examine their own family dynamics more closely.

Internal Pressure and Guilt

Perhaps the most challenging pressure comes from within yourself. During holidays, you might experience intense guilt about maintaining boundaries, worry about missing important moments, or question whether you're being too harsh or unforgiving.

This internal pressure often stems from the positive memories you do have of family celebrations, however few or brief they might have been. The longing for connection and belonging is deeply human, and holidays can amplify this longing, making you wonder if you could somehow recreate those better moments.

You might also experience guilt about the impact of your absence on other family members, particularly children or elderly relatives. The worry that you're depriving grandchildren of relationships with grandparents, or that your aging parents are spending holidays alone, can create intense emotional conflict.

The grief for lost traditions and missed opportunities can also create internal pressure to reconnect. Each holiday that passes without family contact can feel like another opportunity lost forever, especially if family members are aging or in poor health.

Practical Strategies for Holiday Survival

Surviving holidays while maintaining boundaries with toxic family members requires advance planning, emotional preparation, and practical strategies for managing both external pressures and internal conflicts.

Planning Ahead for Emotional Safety

The key to managing holidays successfully is planning ahead rather than making decisions in the emotional intensity of the moment. Start thinking about upcoming holidays several weeks in advance, when you're in a calm, clear mindset rather than feeling pressured by immediate circumstances.

Create a Holiday Boundary Plan:

For each significant holiday or occasion, decide in advance:

- Will you have any contact with toxic family members?
- If so, what type and for how long?
- What topics are off-limits during any contact?
- What will you do if boundaries are violated?
- How will you handle invitations to family gatherings?
- What consequences will you implement if pressure becomes overwhelming?

Identify Your Support System:

Plan who you can reach out to during difficult moments:

- Which friends understand your situation and support your boundaries?
- Do you have access to a therapist or counselor during holiday periods?
- Are there support groups you can connect with?
- Who can you call if you're feeling pressured to violate your boundaries?

Prepare Standard Responses:

Have ready-made responses for common holiday pressures:

- "I've made plans that work best for me this year."
- "I'm celebrating differently this year, but I appreciate your concern."
- "That doesn't work for me, but I hope you have a wonderful celebration."
- "I'm not comfortable discussing my family situation, but thank you for caring."

Creating New Traditions

One of the most powerful ways to reclaim holidays is to create new traditions that reflect your values and bring you genuine joy. These new traditions don't have to be elaborate or expensive; they just need to be meaningful to you and supportive of your well-being.

Solo Celebrations:

If you're spending holidays alone, plan activities that nurture and comfort you:

- Cook a special meal that you actually enjoy, even if it's not a traditional holiday meal
- Watch movies that make you feel good
- Take a nature walk or engage in outdoor activities
- Practice self-care rituals
- Volunteer with organizations that help others during holidays

Chosen Family Gatherings:

Create celebrations with friends, chosen family, or supportive community members:

- Host potluck dinners with friends who also need alternative holiday plans
- Join community celebrations at places of worship, community centers, or cultural organizations
- Organize outdoor activities or travel adventures with supportive friends
- Participate in "Friendsgiving" or other alternative holiday celebrations

Service-Oriented Celebrations:

Many people find deep meaning in spending holidays helping others:

- Volunteer at soup kitchens, homeless shelters, or food banks
- Visit elderly residents at nursing homes
- Participate in toy drives or gift programs for children in need
- Donate time to animal shelters or environmental cleanup projects

Cultural or Spiritual Alternatives:

Explore traditions from other cultures or spiritual practices that resonate with you:

- Learn about how other cultures celebrate similar occasions
- Create rituals based on seasons, nature cycles, or personal spiritual beliefs

- Explore meditation retreats or spiritual communities during holiday periods
- Develop personal practices around gratitude, reflection, or intention-setting

Managing Holiday Communications

If you decide to have limited contact with family members during holidays, having a clear strategy for managing communications can help protect your boundaries while minimizing conflict.

Setting Communication Terms:

- Decide in advance whether you'll send cards, make phone calls, or respond to messages
- Set time limits for any phone conversations
- Choose communication methods that feel the most comfortable to you
- Prepare to end communications that become toxic or boundary-violating

The "Gray Rock" Approach for Holiday Calls:

If you choose to make obligatory holiday phone calls, keep them brief and superficial:

- Stick to neutral topics like weather, general life updates, or safe current events
- Avoid sharing personal information about your relationships, work, or emotional life
- Don't take the bait for arguments or discussions about family conflicts
- Have a predetermined reason to end the call after a set time period

Managing Social Media:

- Consider limiting social media use during intense holiday periods
- Unfollow or hide posts from family members who trigger guilt or anxiety
- Avoid posting about your alternative celebrations if it might invite criticism
- Remember that others' posted celebrations may not reflect their actual experiences

Handling Special Birthdays and Milestones

Significant birthdays, graduations, weddings, births, and other major life events can create particularly intense pressure to reconnect with toxic family members. These occasions feel like they "should" bring families together, and their significance can make your absence feel more noticeable and potentially hurtful to others.

Your Own Significant Birthdays and Achievements

When you reach milestone birthdays or achieve significant life goals, the absence of a family celebration can feel particularly painful. You might find yourself longing for parents who are proud of your accomplishments, siblings who want to celebrate with you, or grandparents who acknowledge your growth and success.

Strategies for Celebrating Your Own Milestones:

- Plan celebrations that reflect your actual preferences rather than family traditions
- Invite people who genuinely support and care about you
- Create documentation of your achievements for your own reflection and pride
- Write yourself a letter acknowledging your growth and accomplishments
- Consider therapy or counseling to process complex emotions around major milestones

Managing Others' Expectations:

- Prepare responses for people who ask if your family will be involved in your celebrations
- Set boundaries with well-meaning friends who want to "fix" your family situation
- Remember that celebrating without toxic family members doesn't diminish your achievements
- Focus on the people who are present rather than those who are absent

Family Members' Significant Events

When toxic family members have birthdays, graduations, weddings, or other major life events, you might face pressure to attend or participate, even if you've maintained no-contact or low-contact boundaries.

Questions to Consider:

- Would attending violate your established boundaries or compromise your well-being?
- Can you participate in a limited way that feels authentic but protected?

- What are the potential consequences of attending versus not attending?
- How will other family relationships be affected by your choice?
- What would you advise a friend in a similar situation?

Alternative Ways to Acknowledge Milestones:

If you choose not to attend family events but want to acknowledge the occasion:

- Send a card with a brief, neutral message
- Make a charitable donation in the person's name
- Send flowers or a gift without attending the celebration
- Acknowledge the event privately through journaling or reflection

Extended Family Events

Weddings, funerals, reunions, and other extended family gatherings can be particularly challenging because they involve multiple family members and may be the only opportunities to see relatives you do want to maintain relationships with.

Strategies for Managing Extended Family Events:

- Attend only if you can maintain your boundaries and have an exit strategy if needed
- Bring a supportive friend or partner who understands your situation
- Stay in a hotel rather than with family members
- Plan specific time limits for your attendance
- Prepare responses for questions about your relationships with toxic family members
- Consider attending only certain portions of the event

Creating Emotional Safety Plans

Having a concrete plan for managing emotional challenges during holidays and special occasions can help you maintain your boundaries while taking care of your mental health.

Before the Holiday/Event

Emotional Preparation:

- Journal about your feelings and expectations for the upcoming occasion
- Practice self-compassion exercises and remind yourself why your boundaries exist
- Review your support system and make sure key people know you might need extra support
- Plan self-care activities before, during, and after the holiday period
- Consider increasing therapy sessions or support group attendance in the weeks leading up to the event

Practical Preparation:

- Finalize your plans for how you'll spend the holiday
- Prepare your physical environment to support your emotional needs
- Stock up on comfort items, good books, favorite foods, or other things that bring you peace
- Make sure you have transportation and accommodations that allow you to leave situations if needed
- Set up accountability with trusted friends who can check in on you

During the Holiday/Event

Staying Grounded:

- Practice mindfulness and grounding techniques when emotions become overwhelming
- Take regular breaks for quiet reflection or brief walks
- Stay hydrated and maintain regular eating patterns
- Limit alcohol consumption, which can lower emotional defenses
- Check in with your support system if you need encouragement or perspective

Managing Unexpected Emotions:

- Allow yourself to feel whatever emotions arise without judgment
- Remember that feeling sad or lonely doesn't mean you made the wrong choice
- When you find yourself stuck in unhelpful thought cycles, try shifting your focus with simple distractions or grounding practices

- Let yourself feel your emotions rather than stuffing them

After the Holiday/Event

Processing and Recovery:

- Journal about your experiences and feelings
- Acknowledge what went well and what you might do differently next time
- Process any guilt or second-guessing with supportive people
- Practice extra self-care in the days following emotional holidays
- Celebrate your success in maintaining boundaries and protecting your well-being

The Long Game: Building Sustainable Holiday Practices

The goal isn't just to survive individual holidays but to develop sustainable practices that allow you to genuinely enjoy these occasions over time. This requires shifting from survival mode to consciously creating holiday experiences that align with your values and support your well-being.

Redefining What Holidays Mean to You

Part of reclaiming holidays involves deciding for yourself what these occasions represent and how you want to experience them. Rather than accepting cultural definitions of what holidays "should" look like, you can create your own meanings that reflect your personal values and spiritual beliefs.

Questions for Reflection:

- What values do I want my holiday celebrations to reflect?
- How do I want to feel during and after holiday celebrations?
- What elements of traditional celebrations bring me genuine joy versus obligation?
- How can I honor the positive aspects of my heritage while protecting myself from toxic dynamics?
- What new traditions might better reflect who I am becoming?

Building Long-term Holiday Resilience

Each holiday season you navigate successfully builds resilience for future occasions. Over time, the intense emotions and pressures often lessen as you establish new patterns and prove to yourself that you can create meaningful celebrations without toxic family involvement.

Developing Holiday Confidence:

- Keep a record of successful holiday strategies to refer to in future years
- Build a collection of meaningful traditions that you can look forward to
- Develop relationships with chosen family members who share your values around celebration
- Create photo albums or journals documenting positive holiday experiences
- Practice gratitude for the progress you've made in creating healthier holiday experiences

Flexibility and Evolution

Remember that your approach to holidays may change over time as you heal and your circumstances evolve. What feels necessary and protective now might feel less important in a few years, or you might develop new strategies that work better for your changing needs.

Stay open to adjusting your approach based on:

- Changes in your emotional resilience and healing progress
- Evolution in family dynamics
- New relationships and chosen family connections
- Changes in practical circumstances
- Growth in your understanding of what truly nourishes you during celebrations

Reflection: Boundary Planning Worksheet

Use this comprehensive planning tool to prepare for upcoming holidays and special occasions while maintaining your emotional safety and honoring your boundaries.

Holiday/Occasion Assessment

Upcoming Event: _____

Date: _____

Historical significance:

- What has this occasion meant in your family?
- What memories do you associate with it?

Emotional triggers associated with this occasion:

- Specific memories: _____
- Sensory triggers: _____
- Family dynamics that typically emerge: _____
- Personal vulnerabilities during this time: _____

Pressure Points Analysis

Rate the intensity of pressure you expect from each source (1 = minimal, 5 = overwhelming):

- Cultural/religious expectations: ____
- Social media comparisons: ____
- Well-meaning friends: ____
- Extended family members: ____
- Direct pressure from toxic family members: ____
- Internal guilt and doubt: ____
- Longing for connection: ____
- Fear of missing important moments: ____

Identify your highest-pressure areas and plan specific strategies for managing them.

Boundary Decision Matrix

For each potentially toxic family member, clarify your boundaries:

- Family Member: _____
- Level of contact I'm comfortable with: _____
- Topics I will/won't discuss: _____
- Time limits for any interaction: _____
- Consequences if boundaries are violated: _____
- Support I need to maintain this boundary: _____

Alternative Celebration Planning

- How I want to spend this occasion:
- Alone time activities that nurture me: _____
- People I want to celebrate with: _____
- New traditions I want to try: _____
- Ways to honor the positive aspects of this occasion: _____
- Service or giving opportunities: _____

Practical arrangements:

- Where I'll spend the day: _____
- What I'll eat: _____
- Who I can call if I need support: _____
- Backup plans if original plans fall through: _____

Communication Strategy

Messages I might need to send:

- To family members: _____
- To extended family/mutual friends: _____
- To my support system: _____

Standard responses I'll use for common pressures:

- "Why aren't you joining the family?" _____
- "Don't you think you should call your mother?" _____
- "It's just one day, can't you make an exception?" _____
- "Your family misses you": _____

Emotional Safety Plan

Warning signs I need extra support:

- Emotional symptoms: _____
- Physical symptoms: _____
- Behavioral changes: _____

My support team:

- Primary support person I can call anytime: _____
- Backup support people: _____
- Professional support available: _____
- Crisis resources if needed: _____

Self-care strategies:

- Before the occasion: _____
- During the occasion: _____
- After the occasion: _____

Grounding techniques for overwhelming moments:

- Breathing exercises: _____
- Sensory grounding: (5 things I can see, 4 I can touch, etc.) _____
- Movement/physical activities: _____
- Comforting objects or spaces: _____

Affirmations and Reminders

Personal affirmations for this occasion:

- "I have the right to celebrate in ways that honor my well-being"
- "My boundaries are acts of self-love, not selfishness"
- "I can create meaningful traditions without toxic family involvement"
- "I am not responsible for others' disappointment with my choices"
- "My healing journey is more important than maintaining harmful traditions"

Reminders of why my boundaries exist:

- Specific examples of past harm during this occasion: _____
- Progress I've made since establishing boundaries: _____
- People who support my boundary decisions: _____
- Values that guide my choices: _____

Success Metrics

How do I know this occasion was successful for me?

- I maintained my boundaries without compromising my values
- I experienced moments of genuine joy or peace
- I felt supported by my chosen celebration approach
- I honored my authentic feelings without judgment
- I practiced good self-care throughout the process

Post-Holiday Reflection

After the occasion, I'll assess:

- What went well and what I want to repeat
- What was challenging and how I might handle it differently
- How my emotions and energy levels were affected
- What I learned about myself and my needs
- How I want to adjust my approach for future occasions

Remember, there's no perfect way to handle holidays and special occasions when you have toxic family members. The goal is to find approaches that protect your well-being while allowing you to experience the joy, connection, and meaning that these occasions can offer. Your celebration doesn't need to look like anyone else's to be valid and meaningful. Trust yourself to create holiday experiences that truly serve your healing and happiness.

Chapter 11: The Fantasy of Reconciliation

Deep in the heart of every person who has distanced themselves from toxic family members lives a persistent hope: maybe this time will be different. Maybe they've finally changed. Maybe they'll acknowledge the harm they've caused. Maybe they'll become the parent, sibling, or family member you've always needed them to be. This hope can feel so real and compelling that it seems cruel to call it a fantasy, yet for many people dealing with truly toxic family dynamics, that's exactly what it is—a beautiful, heartbreaking fantasy that keeps them tethered to relationships that continue to cause harm.

The fantasy of reconciliation is one of the most powerful forces keeping people trapped in toxic family cycles. It's fueled by occasional glimpses of the person's potential, by societal messages about the power of love to heal all wounds, and by our deep human need for connection and belonging. This fantasy whispers that if we just try harder, love more unconditionally, or give one more chance, we can finally have the family relationships we've always longed for.

But hope, while often a source of strength and resilience, can also become a prison when it prevents us from seeing and accepting reality. This chapter explores the difference between healthy hope and destructive fantasy, helps you recognize when hope is serving you versus when it's keeping you stuck, and offers guidance on how to release the fantasy of reconciliation while still honoring your capacity for love and your desire for connection.

The Seductive Nature of Hope

Hope is fundamentally a good thing. It's what drives us to pursue our dreams, work toward positive change, and believe in better possibilities. In healthy relationships, hope motivates us to work through conflicts, forgive mistakes, and grow together. But when applied to genuinely toxic family relationships, hope can become a trap that keeps us vulnerable to ongoing harm.

The hope for reconciliation with toxic family members feels so pure and loving that questioning it can seem cynical or cruel. After all, isn't love supposed to conquer all? Shouldn't we believe in people's capacity to change? Isn't giving up on family members a form of abandonment or betrayal of our deepest values?

These questions touch on fundamental beliefs about love, loyalty, and human nature that most of us hold dear. The fantasy of reconciliation feels noble because it's rooted in genuinely positive values: compassion, forgiveness, unconditional love, and faith in human potential. It's much more comfortable to hold onto this beautiful hope than to accept the painful reality that some people may never change, no matter how much we love them or want them to be different.

The fantasy becomes particularly seductive during moments when the toxic person shows glimpses of their better self. They might apologize after a particularly harmful episode, express regret for past behavior, or show moments of genuine warmth and connection. These glimpses feel like proof that the "real" person is still in there somewhere, just waiting for the right conditions to emerge permanently.

But these moments of hope often come at strategic times—after they've pushed you too far and fear losing you, when they need something from you, or when external circumstances make them temporarily more vulnerable or dependent. The timing isn't accidental; it's often an unconscious manipulation designed to keep you engaged in the relationship. Sometimes it's conscious manipulation.

When Hope Becomes Harmful

While hope can be a powerful force for good, it becomes harmful when it prevents us from seeing and responding to reality appropriately. Hope crosses the line into destructive fantasy when:

It ignores consistent patterns of behavior: Healthy hope is based on evidence of genuine change or at least the person's active efforts to change. Destructive fantasy ignores years or decades of consistent harmful behavior in favor of focusing on brief moments of potential or promises of change that never materialize.

It requires you to sacrifice your well-being: When maintaining hope for reconciliation means exposing yourself to ongoing abuse, manipulation, or emotional harm, that hope is no longer serving your best interests. Healthy relationships don't require you to endure mistreatment in the service of someone else's potential growth.

It becomes more important than your actual lived experience: If you find yourself dismissing or minimizing real harm because it conflicts with your hope for the relationship, that hope has become disconnected from reality. Your actual experiences matter more than your hopes for what the relationship could become.

It prevents you from grieving and moving forward: Holding onto hope for reconciliation can prevent you from processing the grief of accepting that the relationship may never be what you need it to be. This unprocessed grief leaves you trapped in a gray area, unable to accept the loss or move on with your life.

It makes you vulnerable to manipulation: Toxic individuals often become skilled at exploiting your hope for reconciliation. They learn which words, gestures, or behaviors will reignite your hope and use them strategically to regain control or avoid consequences for their actions.

The fantasy of reconciliation can become an addiction of sorts. You become hooked on the intermittent reinforcement of occasional positive interactions, much like a gambler becomes hooked on occasional wins. The unpredictable nature of these positive moments actually makes them more powerful, creating a psychological pattern that's difficult to break.

Recognizing the Difference Between Hope and Harm

Learning to distinguish between healthy hope and destructive fantasy is crucial for making decisions about toxic family relationships that serve your well-being rather than your idealized vision of what could be.

Healthy Hope Includes:

Realistic assessment of the person's actual behavior: Healthy hope acknowledges both positive changes and ongoing problems. It's based on observable evidence rather than wishful thinking.

Respect for your own boundaries and well-being: Healthy hope doesn't require you to sacrifice your mental health, safety, or values in service of someone else's potential change.

Acceptance that change must come from the other person: Healthy hope recognizes that you cannot love, argue, or sacrifice someone into becoming different. Real change comes from within and is demonstrated through consistent actions over time.

Flexibility based on evidence: Healthy hope adjusts based on actual evidence of change or lack thereof. It remains open to positive possibilities while also being willing to accept disappointing realities.

136

Time limits and conditions: Healthy hope often includes specific expectations about what change would look like and reasonable timeframes for seeing evidence of that change.

Destructive Fantasy Includes:

Ignoring consistent patterns of harmful behavior: Destructive fantasy focuses on exceptional moments while dismissing the overwhelming evidence of the person's actual character and choices.

Endless second chances without evidence of change: Destructive fantasy keeps giving opportunities for reconciliation based on promises rather than demonstrated behavioral changes.

Taking responsibility for the other person's growth: Destructive fantasy assumes that your love, patience, or sacrifice can somehow cause the other person to change.

Making excuses for harmful behavior: Destructive fantasy explains away abuse, manipulation, or toxicity as the result of external circumstances, mental health issues, or past trauma, rather than holding the person accountable for their choices. This also includes the excuse that the person did not know any better because that is how they were raised.

No end point or conditions: Destructive fantasy is open-ended hope that doesn't include specific expectations or timeframes, making it impossible to evaluate whether progress is actually being made.

The Cost of Holding On

Maintaining the fantasy of reconciliation with toxic family members comes with significant costs that extend far beyond the specific relationship. These costs can affect every area of your life and impede your overall growth and healing.

Emotional Costs

Ongoing vulnerability to retraumatization: Every time you open yourself to the possibility of reconciliation, you make yourself vulnerable to being hurt again. Each disappointment reinforces old wounds and can set back your healing progress.

Chronic anxiety and hypervigilance: Holding onto hope for reconciliation often means staying emotionally activated and alert to signs of change in the toxic person.

This chronic state of anticipation is exhausting and prevents you from fully relaxing into your own life.

Difficulty forming new attachments: When you're emotionally invested in the fantasy of reconciliation with toxic family members, you may have less emotional energy available for building healthy relationships. Part of your heart remains reserved for family members who consistently disappoint you.

Delayed grief and healing: As long as you're holding onto hope for reconciliation, you can't fully grieve the loss of the relationship you wanted to have. This delayed grief keeps you stuck in earlier stages of healing and prevents you from moving forward.

Relational Costs

Impact on other relationships: The fantasy of reconciliation can affect your other relationships in various ways. You might compare new people to your idealized vision of your family members, have difficulty trusting positive relationships because you're used to disappointment, or struggle to commit fully to your chosen family because you're still emotionally invested in your biological family.

Modeling unhealthy patterns for children: If you have children, maintaining the fantasy of reconciliation with toxic family members can teach them to accept mistreatment in relationships or to believe that love requires enduring harm.

Stress on supportive relationships: Friends, partners, and chosen family members may become frustrated watching you repeatedly get hurt by the same people. Your hope for reconciliation might strain relationships with people who have your best interests at heart.

Practical Costs

Time and energy: The fantasy of reconciliation requires significant emotional energy that could be invested in relationships and activities that actually nurture you. Time spent hoping, planning, and working toward reconciliation is time not spent building the life you actually want and deserve.

Decision-making paralysis: Hope for reconciliation can prevent you from making important life decisions. You might delay moving to a new city, avoid setting firm boundaries, or put off important choices because you're waiting to see if family relationships will improve.

Financial costs: The fantasy of reconciliation can have financial implications if you continue supporting family members financially in hopes of improving the relationship, or if the ongoing stress affects your work performance and career progression.

Spiritual and Identity Costs

Disconnection from your authentic self: Maintaining hope for reconciliation often requires you to suppress your authentic feelings and perceptions in favor of more "loving" or "forgiving" responses. Over time, this can disconnect you from your own truth and intuition.

Confusion about your values: The fantasy of reconciliation can create internal conflict between your values of love and forgiveness and your need for safety and respect. This confusion can make it difficult to make clear decisions about what truly serves your highest good.

Spiritual bypassing: Sometimes the fantasy of reconciliation becomes wrapped up in spiritual or religious beliefs about forgiveness, compassion, and unconditional love in ways that bypass the necessary work of acknowledging harm and protecting yourself.

Common Reconciliation Fantasies

Understanding the specific forms that reconciliation fantasies take can help you recognize when you're operating from fantasy rather than a realistic assessment of the situation.

The Deathbed Confession Fantasy

This fantasy imagines that the toxic person will eventually recognize the harm they've caused, express genuine remorse, and acknowledge your worth and value before they die. In this scenario, years of pain are resolved through a powerful moment of truth-telling and recognition.

While deathbed reconciliations do occasionally happen, they're much rarer than popular culture suggests. Most toxic individuals don't develop sudden self-awareness or accountability in their final days. In fact, serious illness often intensifies existing personality patterns rather than transforming them.

The External Catalyst Fantasy

This fantasy believes that some external event such as a health scare, financial crisis, loss of another relationship, or major life change, will serve as a wake-up call that transforms the toxic person. The fantasy assumes that the right circumstances will finally make them see the light and choose to change.

While external crises can sometimes motivate positive change, they're just as likely to intensify destructive patterns. Crisis often brings out the worst in people with toxic tendencies, as they become more desperate, manipulative, or abusive when they feel their control slipping.

The Grandchildren Fantasy

Many people hope that becoming grandparents will somehow transform their toxic parents into the loving, nurturing caregivers they never were to their own children. The fantasy imagines that the joy and innocence of grandchildren will melt away years of dysfunction and create the family connection that was always missing.

While some people do change their behavior around grandchildren, this change is often superficial and temporary. Toxic individuals may perform the role of loving grandparent for brief periods while maintaining their destructive patterns in other relationships. More concerning, they may attempt to use access to grandchildren as leverage to manipulate their adult children.

The Therapy/Treatment Fantasy

This fantasy believes that if the toxic person would just go to therapy, take medication, attend a support group, or engage in some other form of treatment, they would finally address their issues and become capable of healthy relationships. The fantasy often includes elaborate plans for how to convince them to seek help.

While therapy and treatment can be transformative for people who genuinely want to change, they're ineffective for those who don't see themselves as part of the problem. Toxic individuals often use therapy as another tool for manipulation, becoming skilled at therapeutic language while continuing their harmful behaviors.

The "If I Just..." Fantasy

This is perhaps the most painful fantasy because it places the responsibility for reconciliation on your own behavior. It imagines that if you could just be more patient, understanding, forgiving, or loving enough, you could somehow inspire the toxic person to change. Variations include: "If I just explain it better," "If I just show them how much they're hurting me," or "If I just prove my love..."

This fantasy is particularly destructive because it keeps you trapped in the illusion that you have control over someone else's behavior. It leads to endless self-sacrifice and self-blame when your efforts inevitably fail to produce the desired change.

When Apologies Never Come

One of the most difficult aspects of releasing the fantasy of reconciliation is accepting that the apologies you've longed for may never come. The toxic person may never acknowledge the harm they've caused, express genuine remorse, or take responsibility for their actions. Learning to find peace without these apologies is a crucial part of healing.

The Anatomy of Non-Apologies

Toxic individuals often offer pseudo-apologies that sound like taking responsibility but actually avoid accountability. Learning to recognize these non-apologies can help you avoid mistaking manipulation for genuine change:

"I'm sorry you feel that way" - This places responsibility on your reaction rather than their behavior.

"I'm sorry if I hurt you" - The "if" suggests doubt about whether harm actually occurred.

"I'm sorry, but you..." - Any apology followed by "but" is actually a justification or counter-attack.

"I was going through a hard time" - This explains behavior without taking responsibility for it.

"That's not who I really am" - This suggests their harmful behavior wasn't authentic or intentional.

"I've already apologized for that" - This shuts down ongoing discussion and implies you should be "over it."

"I did the best I could" - This subtly asks for understanding or sympathy while dismissing the pain of the person who was harmed.

"I was a crappy parent" - On the surface, it appears to acknowledge harm, but in reality, it shuts down deeper accountability.

True apologies include specific acknowledgment of harmful behavior, acceptance of responsibility without excuses, expression of genuine remorse, and commitment

141

to different behavior in the future. Anything less is likely manipulation designed to get you to drop the subject and return to the previous dynamic.

Finding Closure Without Apologies

The absence of genuine apologies doesn't mean you can't find closure and peace. Closure is something you create for yourself rather than something someone else gives you.

Write the apology you wish you could receive: Sometimes writing out what you wish the person would say can help you process your need for acknowledgment. This exercise is for you alone and can provide some of the validation you seek.

Give yourself the acknowledgment you need: Practice validating your own experiences and feelings. Tell yourself: "What you experienced was real. You didn't deserve to be treated that way. Your feelings about it are completely valid."

Find witnesses to your truth: Seek out people who can acknowledge your experiences and validate your reality—friends, chosen family, therapists, or support groups where you can share your story and receive the recognition that toxic family members refuse to provide.

Create your own ritual of closure: Design a personal ceremony or practice that symbolizes your decision to stop waiting for apologies that may never come. This might involve writing a letter and burning it, creating artwork that expresses your experience, or planting something to symbolize your growth beyond the relationship.

Accepting Their Limitations

Part of releasing the fantasy of reconciliation involves accepting that the toxic person may not be capable of the kind of self-reflection, accountability, and change that genuine reconciliation would require. This isn't about excusing their behavior or feeling sorry for them. It's about accepting reality so you can make decisions based on what is rather than what you wish could be.

Some people lack the emotional intelligence, empathy, or self-awareness necessary for genuine apologies and behavioral change. Others have personality disorders or mental health conditions that make meaningful change extremely unlikely without intensive, long-term treatment that they must choose for themselves. Still others are so invested in their victim narratives or defensive patterns that acknowledging their harm would threaten their entire sense of self.

Accepting these limitations doesn't mean you're giving up on the person or becoming cynical about human nature. It means you're being realistic about the actual person in front of you rather than the idealized version you wish existed. This acceptance can actually be liberating. It frees you from the impossible task of trying to change someone else and allows you to focus on what you can control: your own healing, growth, and choices about how to respond to their limitations.

The Grief of Letting Go

Releasing the fantasy of reconciliation involves a profound grief process that can feel as intense as mourning a death. In many ways, you are mourning deaths, the death of hope, the death of the relationship you wanted, the death of the parent or family member you needed them to be.

This grief is often disenfranchised, meaning it's not widely recognized or validated by society. People may not understand why you're grieving when the person is still alive, or they may try to rush you through the grief process by suggesting you should "just move on" or "focus on the positive." But this grief is real and necessary, and it deserves the same respect and patience you would give any other significant loss.

Stages of Grieving the Fantasy

The grief of letting go of reconciliation hopes often follows patterns similar to other grief processes, though not necessarily in linear stages.

Denial: "This can't be the end. There must be a way to work things out. They'll change eventually."

Anger: "How dare they refuse to acknowledge what they've done. I've given them so many chances. They're selfish and cruel."

Bargaining: "If I just try one more approach, maybe I can get through to them. Maybe if I change my tactics..."

Depression: "I'll never have the family I wanted. I've wasted so much time and energy. What's wrong with me that I can't make this work?"

Acceptance: "This is who they are and who they've chosen to be. I can love them and still choose to protect myself from their toxicity."

Honoring Your Grief

Allow yourself to feel the full range of emotions that come with letting go of reconciliation hopes. Sadness, anger, relief, fear, and even guilt are all normal responses to this kind of loss.

Create rituals or practices that honor both what you're releasing and what you're choosing instead. This might involve writing letters you don't send, journaling, creating artwork, or having conversations with trusted friends about your decision.

Be patient with the process. Grief doesn't follow a timeline, and you may cycle through different feelings many times before reaching a stable sense of acceptance.

Seek support from people who understand your situation and can validate your decision to prioritize your well-being over reconciliation hopes.

I believe that grief is love with nowhere to go. The intensity of your grief reflects the depth of your caring, not a weakness or failure on your part.

Building a Life Beyond the Fantasy

Once you've begun the process of releasing the fantasy of reconciliation, you can start building a life that's based on reality rather than hope for something that may never come. This involves redirecting the energy you've been putting into reconciliation hopes toward relationships and activities that actually nourish you.

Redirecting Your Love

The love you've been directing toward toxic family members in hopes of reconciliation doesn't disappear when you accept that the relationship may not change. That love can be redirected toward people and causes that can actually receive and benefit from it.

Invest in relationships with people who can reciprocate your caring and who treat you with respect and kindness.

Consider mentoring or supporting others who have been through similar experiences with toxic family dynamics.

Redirect your caregiving energy toward causes, animals, or communities that can benefit from your compassion.

Practice self-love and self-care with the same intensity you once directed toward hoping for family reconciliation.

Creating New Meaning

The meaning you found in hoping for reconciliation, the sense of purpose, the belief in love's power, the faith in human potential, can be channeled into other areas of your life.

Focus on relationships where your love and effort create positive change rather than relationships where you're constantly swimming upstream.

Find meaning in your own healing journey and the ways your growth can inspire others.

Engage in work or causes that align with your values and allow you to make a positive impact.

Develop spiritual practices or philosophical frameworks that help you find meaning beyond family relationships.

Building New Traditions and Connections

Instead of organizing your life around the hope of family reconciliation, you can create new patterns and traditions based on the relationships and values that actually serve your well-being.

Develop traditions with chosen family that reflect your authentic preferences rather than obligatory family patterns.

Create celebration practices that honor your growth and healing rather than trying to recreate family dynamics that never worked.

Build community connections based on shared interests, values, or experiences rather than blood relationships.

Establish a lifestyle that prioritizes your mental health and authentic desires rather than family expectations or hopes.

Reflection: Radical Acceptance Journaling

Use these prompts to explore your relationship with reconciliation fantasies and practice accepting reality while honoring your capacity for love.

Examining Your Reconciliation Fantasies

Identifying Your Specific Fantasies:

- What do you imagine would happen if your toxic family member truly changed?

- How do you picture the conversation or moment when they finally "see the light"?

- What external event do you sometimes hope will transform them?

- What do you imagine you could do or say that would finally get through to them?

- How do you picture your life be different if reconciliation had happened?

Tracing the Origins:

- When did you first start hoping for this kind of change from this person?

- What moments or glimpses have kept this hope alive?

- What messages support your belief that reconciliation is possible or necessary?

- How has this hope served you in the past? What needs has it met?

Reality Testing

Evidence Assessment:

- What concrete evidence do I have that this person is capable of the change I'm hoping for?

- How long have I been hoping for this change? What has actually changed in that time?

- When this person has apologized before, what happened afterward?

- What patterns of behavior have remained consistent regardless of circumstances?

- How has this person responded when I've clearly expressed my needs or boundaries?

Cost-Benefit Analysis:

- What has maintaining this hope cost me emotionally?

- How has it affected my other relationships?

- What opportunities have I missed while waiting for reconciliation?

- How much energy have I invested in this hope versus in relationships that actually nurture me?

- What would I do differently if I fully accepted that reconciliation might never happen?

Grieving the Fantasy

Letter to Your Hope:

Write a letter to your hope for reconciliation, acknowledging both what it has given you and what it has cost you:

"Dear Hope for Reconciliation with [name],

You have been with me for [time period], and you have given me...

But you have also cost me...

I am grateful for the ways you have shown me my capacity for love and my desire for connection, but I am ready to...

Thank you for... and goodbye to..."

What You're Actually Mourning:

- I am grieving the parent/sibling/family member I needed them to be
- I am mourning the childhood/family experience I never had
- I am sad about the time and energy I've spent hoping for something that may never come
- I am letting go of the vision of our family being happy and healthy together
- I am accepting that they may never understand or acknowledge the harm they've caused

Accepting Reality

Completing These Statements:

- "The truth about [person's name] is that they..."
- "Despite my hopes, they have consistently..."
- "I cannot change the fact that..."
- "Accepting this reality means I can..."
- "I am allowed to love them and still..."

Radical Acceptance Affirmations:

Choose the affirmations that resonate with your situation:

- "I can love someone and still protect myself from their toxicity"
- "Accepting reality is not giving up on love, it's choosing to love wisely"
- "I don't need their change or acknowledgment to heal and move forward"
- "My worth is not dependent on their ability to see and value me"
- "I can grieve what never was while celebrating what I'm creating now"

Redirecting Your Love

Where Your Love Can Flourish:

- People in my life who can actually receive and reciprocate my love: _____
- Causes or communities that would benefit from my caring: _____
- Ways I can show love to myself: _____
- New traditions or practices I want to create: _____
- Relationships I want to invest more deeply in: _____

Creating New Meaning:

- What values do I want to prioritize now that I'm not focused on reconciliation?
- How do I want to spend the emotional energy I've been putting into reconciliation hopes?
- What dreams or goals have I put on hold while hoping for family change?
- What kind of legacy do I want to create with my life?
- How can my experience with toxic family dynamics help others?

Moving Forward Plan

Immediate Steps:

- I will stop checking their social media/asking others about them
- I will redirect conversations that fuel reconciliation fantasies
- I will invest more time and energy in relationships that actually nourish me
- I will practice self-compassion when grief waves hit
- I will seek support from people who understand my decision

Long-term Vision:

- In one year, I want to feel...
- The relationships I want to prioritize are...
- The new traditions I want to establish are...
- The personal growth I want to focus on includes...
- I will know I've successfully let go of the reconciliation fantasy when...

Honoring Both Love and Boundaries

Integration Practice:

Write a statement that honors both your capacity for love and your need for protection.

"I deeply love [person's name] AND I choose to protect myself from their toxicity. My love for them doesn't require me to accept harmful behavior. I can hold both love and boundaries. I can grieve what our relationship never was while celebrating my strength in choosing health and healing."

Remember, letting go of the fantasy of reconciliation is not about becoming hard-hearted or giving up on love. It's about directing your love more wisely toward relationships and situations where it can actually create positive change and mutual flourishing. Your capacity for love is a beautiful gift, and you deserve to share it with people who can truly receive and appreciate it.

Chapter 12: Talking to Others Who Don't Understand

One of the most isolating aspects of cutting ties with toxic family members is the lack of understanding and support from others in your life. Well-meaning friends, colleagues, acquaintances, and even other family members often respond to news of your estrangement with confusion, judgment, or attempts to "help" by encouraging reconciliation. Their responses can leave you feeling defensive, misunderstood, and questioning your own decisions.

The truth is, choosing to step away from family is something most people can't comprehend unless they've known the weight of toxic family dynamics firsthand. Their incomprehension isn't necessarily malicious. It often comes from their own fortunate experiences with relatively functional families, cultural conditioning about the sacred nature of family bonds, or genuine concern for your well-being. However, their lack of understanding can still be deeply hurtful and can add an additional layer of stress to an already difficult situation.

This chapter will help you navigate these challenging conversations with confidence and clarity. We'll explore why people struggle to understand family estrangement, how to respond to common reactions and questions, and strategies for protecting your energy while maintaining relationships with people who may never fully grasp your choices. Most importantly, we'll help you develop your own "explainer script" that honors your truth while setting appropriate boundaries around what you're willing to discuss.

Why People Don't Understand

Understanding why others struggle to comprehend family estrangement can help you respond with patience and clarity rather than defensiveness or anger. Their lack of understanding usually stems from several common factors that have nothing to do with your actual situation or the validity of your choices.

Limited Personal Experience

Most people who question your decision to limit contact with family members have never experienced severe family toxicity themselves. Their families may have had conflicts, disagreements, or even significant problems, but these issues were ultimately resolvable through communication, compromise, or time. Their frame of reference for family conflict includes making up after arguments, working through differences, and maintaining relationships despite occasional hurt feelings.

When someone has only experienced normal family dysfunction, the kind that can be resolved through better communication or therapy, they naturally assume that all family problems are solvable if people just try hard enough. They can't imagine circumstances where love and effort aren't enough to repair a family relationship because that's never been their reality.

Their suggestions often reflect this limited experience: "Have you tried talking to them about how you feel?" "Maybe you could suggest family therapy?" "Don't you think you should try harder to work it out?" These suggestions aren't necessarily wrong for normal family conflicts, but they demonstrate a fundamental misunderstanding of toxic family dynamics where the problem isn't poor communication— it's deliberately harmful behavior.

Cultural and Religious Programming

Most cultures and religions have strong teachings about family loyalty, honoring parents, and maintaining family bonds regardless of circumstances. These messages are so deeply ingrained that many people have never questioned them or considered that there might be exceptions to these rules.

Religious teachings about forgiveness, turning the other cheek, and honoring your father and mother can create particularly strong resistance to understanding family estrangement. People may genuinely believe they're helping you by encouraging reconciliation, thinking they're guiding you toward spiritual growth or moral behavior.

Cultural messages about family being "everything" or "all you have" can also make it difficult for people to understand why you would choose to distance yourself from biological relatives. In many cultures, family estrangement is seen as shameful or evidence of personal failure rather than a necessary act of self-preservation.

Discomfort with Their Own Family Dynamics

Sometimes people's resistance to understanding your choices stems from their own unexamined family relationships. If they've tolerated dysfunction, abuse, or toxicity in their own families, accepting that you have the right to set boundaries might force them to question their own choices.

They might worry that if your boundaries are valid, then perhaps they should also be setting firmer limits with their own problematic family members. This realization can feel threatening, especially if they're not ready or able to make changes in their own lives. It's often easier to convince you that you're wrong than to examine their own family dynamics.

Fear of Family Breakdown

Your decision to limit contact with family members might trigger fears in others about the stability of families in general. If someone deeply values family unity and sees it as one of society's foundational structures, your estrangement might feel threatening to their worldview.

They might worry that accepting your choice somehow endorses family breakdown or gives others "permission" to abandon their family responsibilities. Their attempts to convince you to reconcile might be more about preserving their beliefs than about your specific situation.

Projection of Their Own Values and Needs

Many people assume that everyone shares their values and needs around family connection. Someone who derives great meaning and comfort from family relationships might not be able to imagine feeling differently, even under harmful circumstances.

They might think they're being helpful by encouraging you to preserve something they see as precious and irreplaceable. Their inability to understand your choice often reflects their projection of their own values rather than any real understanding of your experience.

Common Responses and What They Really Mean

Learning to decode the common responses people have to news of family estrangement can help you understand what's really driving their reactions and respond more effectively.

"But They're Your Family"

This response reflects the belief that blood relationships automatically deserve loyalty and tolerance regardless of behavior. People who say this often genuinely cannot conceive of circumstances where family connection wouldn't be worth preserving.

What they're really saying: Family relationships are sacred and should be maintained at all costs. Blood bonds create obligations that supersede personal well-being.

The assumption behind it: All family problems can be worked through if people try hard enough. No family relationship is so damaged that it can't be repaired with sufficient love and effort.

"You Only Get One Mother/Father"

This response emphasizes the irreplaceable nature of parent-child relationships while ignoring the quality of those relationships. It assumes that scarcity makes something valuable regardless of its actual impact on your life.

What they're really saying: Because you can't replace your parents, you should tolerate whatever treatment they give you. The uniqueness of the relationship makes it precious by default.

The assumption behind it: Any relationship with your parents is better than no relationship. You'll regret losing this connection when they're gone.

"Nobody's Perfect"

This response minimizes the severity of toxic behavior by framing it as a normal human imperfection. It suggests that you're being unreasonably demanding or intolerant of normal human flaws.

What they're really saying: You should lower your expectations and accept that everyone has problems. Your standards for treatment are too high.

The assumption behind it: The behavior you're describing is just a normal human imperfection rather than genuinely harmful toxicity. You're being too sensitive or demanding.

"They Did Their Best"

This response asks you to focus on intention rather than impact, suggesting that good intentions excuse harmful behavior. It often comes from people who believe parents automatically deserve credit for effort regardless of results.

What they're really saying: You should be grateful for whatever love and care you received, even if it came with significant harm. Parents' limitations excuse their failures.

The assumption behind it: Parents naturally love their children, and any harm they cause is unintentional or due to circumstances beyond their control.

"Life Is Too Short"

This response uses the reality of mortality to pressure immediate reconciliation without addressing whether that reconciliation would be healthy or genuine. It creates urgency around a decision that should be made carefully.

What they're really saying: You should prioritize time with family over your emotional well-being because death could separate you at any moment.

The assumption behind it: Any time with family is valuable time, regardless of the quality of those interactions or their impact on your mental health.

"They Must Miss You"

This response focuses on the family member's possible feelings while ignoring your actual experience of harm. It asks you to prioritize others' emotions over your own well-being.

What they're really saying: You should consider how your absence affects your family members and prioritize their feelings over your own needs.

The assumption behind it: Your family members have good intentions, and their distress about your absence proves they care about you.

"Maybe They've Changed"

This response reflects hope that toxic people naturally grow and change over time without addressing whether there's any evidence of actual transformation. It encourages you to risk retraumatization based on possibility rather than evidence.

What they're really saying: You should give your family members another chance because people can change, regardless of their history or any evidence of actual change.

The assumption behind it: Time automatically leads to personal growth, and people learn from their mistakes even without consequences or intervention.

Strategies for Responding

Having prepared responses for common reactions can help you navigate these conversations with confidence while protecting your energy and maintaining your boundaries.

The Brief and Boundaries Approach

Sometimes the best response is to keep your explanation brief and immediately set boundaries around further discussion.

- "We have different perspectives on family relationships, and this isn't something I'm comfortable discussing."

- "I've made the decision that's healthiest for me, and I'd appreciate your respect for my personal choice."

- "This is a private family matter and I'm not going to get into details about it."

- "I understand this might be hard to understand, but I need you to trust that I know what's best for my situation."

This approach works well with acquaintances, colleagues, or people you don't want to have deeper conversations with about your personal life.

The Educational Approach

With close friends or family members who genuinely want to understand, you might choose to provide more education about toxic family dynamics.

- "When I say 'family problems,' I'm talking about patterns of abuse and manipulation that went on for years. This isn't about normal family conflict that can be resolved through better communication."

- "I understand it's hard to imagine because you have a healthy family, but some family relationships are genuinely harmful to people's mental health and well-being."

- "The difference between a difficult family member and a toxic one is that toxic people consistently refuse to take responsibility for harmful behavior and continue to cause damage despite clear feedback about the impact of their actions."

The Redirection Approach

Sometimes you can acknowledge their concern while redirecting the conversation away from debate about your choices.

- "I appreciate that you care about me, but I've thought about this carefully and I'm comfortable with my decision. How are things going with [change subject]?"

- "Thanks for your concern. I'm actually doing really well and focusing on [positive aspects of your life]. Speaking of which, [redirect conversation]."

- "I know it seems unusual, but I'm in a much better place emotionally since I made this decision. Let me tell you about [positive development in your life]."

The Firm Boundary Approach

When people persist in trying to convince you to reconcile or continue to question your judgment, you may need to be more direct.

- "I need you to stop trying to convince me to reconcile. This decision is not open for debate."

- "If you can't respect my boundaries around this topic, we'll need to limit our conversations to other subjects."

- "I'm going to end this conversation if you keep pushing me to change my mind about my family situation."

The Empathetic but Firm Approach

This approach acknowledges their good intentions while maintaining your boundaries.

- "I can see that you care about me and want me to be happy, which I appreciate. What would make me happy is having your support for the difficult but necessary decision I've made."

- "I know this is coming from a place of love, but what I need from you is trust that I know my own situation better than anyone else."

- "I understand this might trigger concerns about your own family relationships, but my situation is unique and requires different solutions than what might work for others."

Choosing What to Disclose and to Whom

Not everyone in your life needs or deserves detailed explanations about your family situation. Learning to discern who gets what level of information can help you protect your energy while maintaining important relationships.

Categories of People in Your Life

Inner Circle: These are people who have earned your trust and who consistently support your well-being. They might include your closest friends, chosen family, romantic partners, or therapists. These people generally deserve honest explanations about your family situation if you choose to share.

Middle Circle: These are people you care about and interact with regularly, but who don't necessarily need detailed information about your personal life. They might include good friends, some family members, or close colleagues. With these people, you can choose to share general information while maintaining boundaries around details.

Outer Circle: These are acquaintances, casual friends, distant relatives, or colleagues with whom you have limited relationships. These people generally don't need explanations about your family choices, and you can use brief, polite responses to deflect their questions.

Hostile or Unsafe People: These are people who have shown they cannot be trusted with personal information or who might use your vulnerabilities against you. This might include family members who side with toxic relatives, people who have betrayed your trust before, or individuals who seem to thrive on drama or gossip.

Information Levels

Full Disclosure: Detailed explanation of the abuse, toxicity, or harmful patterns that led to your decision. This level of sharing is appropriate only for your inner circle and only when you choose to provide it.

General Explanation: Basic information about needing to protect your mental health by limiting contact with family members who are harmful to your well-being. This might include mentioning "toxic family dynamics" or "unhealthy patterns" without specific details.

Minimal Information: Simple statements about having made different choices about family relationships or needing space from certain family members. This level is appropriate for most middle and outer circle relationships.

No Information: Simply declining to discuss your family situation or redirecting conversations away from the topic. This is completely appropriate for outer circle relationships and hostile people.

Factors to Consider in Disclosure Decisions

Their demonstrated ability to support you: Have they shown understanding and support around other difficult topics in your life?

Their relationship to your family: Are they connected to your family members in ways that might create conflicts of loyalty or opportunities for information to be shared inappropriately?

Your emotional capacity: Do you have the energy to potentially educate them or handle their reaction, or are you feeling too vulnerable for that conversation?

The potential consequences: What might happen if they don't respond well or if they share this information with others?

Your motivation: Are you sharing because you want support and understanding, or because you feel pressured to justify your choices?

Developing Your Personal Explainer Script

Having a prepared script can help you feel more confident in conversations about your family situation while ensuring you communicate your boundaries clearly and consistently.

Components of an Effective Script

Acknowledgment: Briefly acknowledge that your choice might seem unusual or concerning to them.

Boundary: Make it clear what you are and aren't willing to discuss.

Redirection: Offer an alternative focus for the conversation or relationship.

Appreciation: Thank them for their concern while maintaining your position.

Sample Scripts for Different Situations

For Close Friends Who Want to Understand: "I know it might seem strange that I don't talk to my [family member], but I made this decision to protect my mental health after years of trying to make the relationship work. The situation was genuinely harmful to my well-being, and I'm much healthier and happier since I established these boundaries. I appreciate your concern for me, and what would help most is knowing you support my right to make decisions about my own relationships."

For Acquaintances or Casual Friends: "We have different perspectives on family relationships, and I've made the choice that works best for me. I'd rather not get into the details, but I appreciate your concern. How are things going with your family?"

For Persistent Questioners: "I understand this might be hard to understand, but I need you to trust that I know my situation better than anyone else. I'm not comfortable discussing the details, and I need you to respect that boundary. Can we talk about something else?"

For Religious or Cultural Pressure: "I appreciate that your faith/culture emphasizes family unity, and I respect those values. In my situation, I've found that protecting myself from harmful relationships is also a way of honoring the life and well-being that I believe God/the universe wants for me. I hope you can respect that I've made this decision thoughtfully and with careful consideration of my values."

For Family Members: "I know my choice affects the whole family, and I'm sorry if that creates difficulties for you. This wasn't a decision I made lightly, but it's necessary for my well-being. I hope we can maintain our relationship while respecting that I need to handle my other family relationships differently than you might choose to handle yours."

Customizing Your Script

Consider your communication style: Are you naturally direct or more diplomatic? Choose a language that feels authentic to how you normally communicate.

Think about your audience: What values and concerns are likely to be most important to the specific people you're talking to?

Include your bottom lines: What are you absolutely not willing to discuss or negotiate about?

Prepare for follow-up questions: What are people most likely to ask after your initial response, and how will you handle those questions?

157

Practice saying it: Rehearse your script so it feels natural and you can deliver it confidently even when you're feeling emotional or defensive.

Adjusting Your Script Over Time

Your explainer script may evolve as you become more confident in your choices and as your healing progresses. You might find that you're comfortable sharing more details as you become stronger, or conversely, that you prefer to share less as you realize you don't need others to understand or validate your choices.

Pay attention to:

- Which responses feel most authentic and effective for you
- How different people respond to different approaches
- What level of explanation leaves you feeling empowered versus drained
- Whether your comfort level with disclosure changes over time
- What boundaries do you want to maintain around follow-up conversations

Protecting Your Energy

Conversations about family estrangement can be emotionally draining, especially when you encounter judgment, pressure, or a lack of understanding. Protecting your energy during and after these conversations is crucial for maintaining your well-being.

Before Difficult Conversations

Prepare emotionally: Remind yourself of your reasons for your boundaries and affirm your right to make these choices.

Set realistic expectations: Don't expect to change everyone's mind or receive universal understanding.

Plan your responses: Know in advance how you'll handle common reactions and what your boundaries are around the conversation.

Choose your timing: Have these conversations when you're feeling strong and centered rather than when you're already stressed or vulnerable.

Arrange support: Let someone in your support system know you might need encouragement or processing after the conversation.

During the Conversation

Stay grounded: Use breathing techniques or other grounding strategies if you start feeling defensive or overwhelmed.

Stick to your script: Return to your prepared responses rather than getting drawn into debates or justifications.

Set time limits: It's okay to say, "I only have a few minutes to talk about this" or "I need to end this conversation now."

Don't over-explain: The more you explain, the more opportunities you give for argument or debate.

Trust your instincts: If the conversation becomes hostile or unproductive, you have the right to end it.

After the Conversation

Process your feelings: Journal, talk to a trusted friend, or engage in other activities that help you process any emotions that come up.

Practice self-care: Engage in activities that restore your sense of peace and self-worth.

Reassess the relationship: Consider whether this person can respect your boundaries around this topic or if you need to adjust your level of sharing with them.

Celebrate your courage: Acknowledge that standing up for your choices takes strength, especially in the face of misunderstanding or pressure.

Building Your Support Network

Not everyone will understand your choices, but some people will. Building relationships with people who can support your decisions about family is crucial for maintaining your confidence and emotional well-being.

Finding Your People

Support groups: Online or in-person support groups for people with similar experiences can provide understanding and validation that's difficult to find elsewhere.

Therapy: Individual therapy can provide professional support and help you process the challenges of navigating relationships while maintaining family boundaries.

Chosen family: Friends who become like family can provide the connection and support that biological family members cannot.

Online communities: Social media groups, forums, or other online spaces focused on family estrangement or toxic family dynamics can provide community and resources.

Books and resources: Reading others' stories and expert perspectives can help you feel less alone and provide language for your experiences.

Nurturing Supportive Relationships

Be clear about your needs: Let supportive people know what kind of support is most helpful to you.

Show appreciation: Thank people who respect your boundaries and support your choices.

Offer reciprocal support: Be available to support others in their challenges as they support you in yours.

Set boundaries even with supporters: You don't owe anyone detailed explanations just because they're supportive.

Invest your energy wisely: Spend more time and emotional energy on relationships that nourish you rather than those that drain you.

Reflection: Writing Your Own "Explainer" Script

Use this exercise to develop personalized responses for different people and situations in your life.

Audience Analysis

List the different categories of people who might ask about your family situation:

- *Inner Circle (deserves full honesty if you choose to share):*
- Middle Circle (general explanations are appropriate):
- Outer Circle (minimal information):
- People to avoid sharing with:

Common Questions You Face

What questions do you get most often about your family situation?

1.
2.
3.
4.
5.

What assumptions do people make that are most frustrating or hurtful?

1.
2.
3.
4.
5.

Your Core Messages

Complete these statements to clarify your core messages.

"The most important thing for people to understand about my situation is..."

"I need people to respect..."

"What would be most helpful from others is..."

"I am not comfortable discussing..."

"What I want people to know about my well-being is..."

Script Development

For Inner Circle - Detailed Response: "When people I trust want to understand my family situation, I can say: [Write a 2-3 sentence explanation that includes key information about your boundaries and your well-being]"

For Middle Circle - General Response: "When friends or acquaintances ask about my family, I can say: [Write a 1-2 sentence response that acknowledges their concern while maintaining appropriate boundaries]"

For Outer Circle - Minimal Response: "When acquaintances or colleagues ask about my family, I can say: [Write a brief response that deflects the question politely]"

For Persistent Questions: "When people won't let the topic go, I can say: [Write a firm but polite response that sets a clear boundary]"

For Pressure to Reconcile: "When people try to convince me to reconcile, I can say: [Write a response that acknowledges their concern while maintaining your position]"

Boundary Phrases

Practice these phrases for setting boundaries in conversations:

- "I appreciate your concern, but..."
- "This isn't something I'm comfortable discussing..."
- "I need you to respect my decision about..."
- "I'd prefer to talk about..."
- "That's not something I'm going to change my mind about..."
- "I need to end this conversation if..."

Follow-Up Responses

For each of your main scripts, prepare responses to likely follow-up questions or comments:

If they say "But they're your family":

If they say, "Maybe you should try therapy/talking to them":

If they say, "You might regret this someday":

If they say "Nobody's perfect":

If they share their own family conflict stories:

Self-Care Planning

- After difficult conversations about family, I will:
- People I can talk to for support and validation:
- Reminders I need when I'm feeling defensive or misunderstood:

Practice and Refinement

Test your scripts with safe people first:

- Practice with a therapist, trusted friend, or support group
- Notice which phrases feel most natural and confident
- Pay attention to which responses leave you feeling empowered versus drained
- Adjust your language based on what feels most authentic to you

Track what works:

- Keep notes on which responses are most effective with different types of people
- Notice patterns in the questions you receive
- Refine your scripts based on actual conversations
- Celebrate successful boundary-setting conversations

Remember, you don't need everyone to understand your choices about family relationships. Your job is not to convince others or to justify your decisions to people who haven't lived your experience. Your job is to protect your well-being, honor your truth, and build a life that reflects your values and supports your healing. The right people will respect your boundaries even if they don't fully understand your situation, and those are the relationships worth nurturing and protecting.

Chapter 13: Building Your Chosen Family

One of the most transformative aspects of healing from toxic family relationships is discovering that family isn't just about blood; it's about love, respect, support, and genuine care. When your biological family cannot or will not provide the connection you need, you have the power to create a chosen family that does. This chosen family can become a source of strength, joy, and belonging that may surpass anything you experienced in your family of origin.

Building a chosen family isn't about replacing your biological relatives with substitutes. It's about expanding your definition of family to include people who treat you with the love and respect you deserve. These relationships are based on mutual choice, shared values, and genuine affection rather than obligation or genetics. They represent what family relationships can be when they're healthy, supportive, and life-giving. You don't always choose your chosen family. Sometimes they choose you.

This chapter will guide you through the process of identifying, building, and nurturing chosen family relationships. We'll explore what makes someone chosen family material, how to develop these deep connections, and how to create traditions and bonds that provide the sense of belonging that healthy families offer. Most importantly, we'll help you understand that the chosen family isn't a consolation prize—it's often a richer, more authentic experience of family than many people ever have.

Understanding Chosen Family

Chosen family represents a fundamental shift in how we think about family relationships. Instead of accepting that family is something that happens to you based on genetics or marriage, chosen family recognizes that the most meaningful family relationships are often those we consciously create and nurture.

What Makes Someone Chosen Family

Chosen family members are distinguished by several key characteristics that may have been absent in your biological family relationships.

Mutual respect and acceptance: They see and appreciate you for who you truly are, not who they want you to be or who they think you should become. They celebrate your authentic self rather than trying to change or control you.

Emotional safety: You can be vulnerable with them without fear of having that vulnerability used against you later. They hold your secrets, support you through difficulties, and create space for your full range of emotions.

163

Reciprocal care: The relationship involves give and take, with both people showing up for each other in times of need. There's a natural flow of support that doesn't require keeping score or maintaining perfect balance.

Shared values or deep understanding: While you don't have to agree on everything, you share core values about how people should be treated or have a deep understanding of each other's perspectives and experiences.

Consistent presence: They show up reliably over time, through both good times and challenges. Their presence in your life isn't conditional on your performance or their convenience.

Growth orientation: They support your growth and healing rather than trying to keep you stuck in old patterns. They encourage your progress and celebrate your positive changes.

Boundary respect: They understand and honor your boundaries without making you feel guilty or demanding explanations. They also maintain healthy boundaries of their own.

Types of Chosen Family Relationships

Chosen family can take many different forms, depending on your needs, life circumstances, and the people who come into your life.

The Mentor Figure: Someone older or more experienced who provides guidance, wisdom, and parental-type support. This might be a teacher, boss, therapist, spiritual leader, or family friend who takes a genuine interest in your well-being and growth.

The Sibling Friend: A peer who becomes like a brother or sister to you, sharing inside jokes, family-like intimacy, and unconditional support. These relationships often involve knowing each other deeply and being able to be completely authentic together.

The Chosen Parent: Someone who provides the nurturing, guidance, and unconditional positive regard that healthy parents offer. This might be an older friend, mentor, or community member who treats you with the care you needed from your biological parents.

The Chosen Child: Sometimes you become a parental figure to someone else who needs support, guidance, or nurturing. This might be a younger friend, mentee, or community member whom you help guide through life challenges.

The Soul Friend: Someone who understands you at a deep level and with whom you share profound emotional intimacy. These relationships often transcend typical friendship categories and feel like true kinship of the spirit.

The Family Unit: A group of friends who function together like a family unit, sharing holidays, major life events, and ongoing daily support. These groups often develop their own traditions and ways of caring for each other.

The Difference Between Friends and Chosen Family

While all chosen family members might start as friends, not all friends become chosen family. The distinction lies in the depth of commitment, level of intimacy, and sense of permanence in the relationship.

Friends are people you enjoy spending time with, share interests with, and care about. The relationship may be somewhat situational (work friends, hobby friends) or dependent on external circumstances.

Chosen family represents a deeper level of commitment and intimacy. These are people you would call in a crisis, who know your deepest struggles and greatest joys, and with whom you expect to maintain a relationship regardless of changing circumstances.

The progression from friend to chosen family often happens gradually as trust deepens, intimacy increases, and you discover that you can count on each other through various life challenges. Not every friendship needs to become your chosen family, and recognizing the difference can help you appreciate various types of relationships for what they offer.

Identifying Potential Chosen Family Members

Building a chosen family starts with recognizing the people in your life who already demonstrate chosen family qualities, as well as being open to new people who might become part of your chosen family over time.

Recognizing Existing Chosen Family

You may already have chosen family members in your life without having named them as such. These people might be:

The friend who always answers your calls: The person who consistently shows up when you need them, regardless of their own circumstances or convenience.

The person who celebrates your wins: Someone who genuinely rejoices in your successes without jealousy or competition, and who remembers important events in your life.

The one who sees through your masks: Someone who recognizes when you're struggling even when you're trying to hide it, and who gently creates space for your authentic feelings.

The person who feels like home: Being with them feels comfortable, safe, and restorative. You can relax and be yourself without performance or pretense.

The one who has earned your trust: Through consistent actions over time, they've proven they can be trusted with your vulnerabilities, secrets, and genuine self.

Qualities to Look for in New Relationships

As you meet new people and develop friendships, certain qualities suggest someone might have chosen family potential. Some of the qualities to look for are:

Emotional intelligence: They understand and can navigate emotions, both their own and others', with maturity and skill. They can handle conflict constructively and communicate about difficult topics.

Capacity for depth: They're interested in and capable of deeper conversations and connections, not just surface-level interactions. They want to know who you really are, not just the version of you that's easy or convenient.

Reliability: Their actions match their words consistently over time. When they say they'll do something or be somewhere, they follow through.

Growth mindset: They're committed to their own growth and healing, and they support yours. They don't try to keep you stuck in old patterns that serve their needs.

Healthy boundaries: They maintain appropriate boundaries in their relationships and respect others' boundaries without taking them personally.

Reciprocal interest: They're as interested in supporting and knowing you as they are in being supported and known by you.

Red Flags to Avoid

Some people might seem appealing as potential chosen family but actually recreate patterns from toxic biological families. Some of the red flags to look for are:

They love-bomb initially: They shower you with attention and affection early in the relationship, making you feel special and chosen, but this intensity often masks underlying instability or manipulation.

They have boundary issues: They push against your limits, ignore your "no," or expect you to tolerate behavior you've clearly indicated is unacceptable.

They're only available when convenient: They show up when they need something or when it's easy for them, but disappear when you need support or when the relationship requires effort.

They compete with you: They can't genuinely celebrate your successes, feel threatened by your growth, or try to one-up your experiences rather than supporting you.

They try to fix or change you: Instead of accepting who you are, they have an agenda for who you should become and pressure you to meet their expectations.

They recreate family drama: They bring the same types of conflict, manipulation, or dysfunction that characterized your toxic family relationships.

Nurturing Deep Connections

Building chosen family relationships requires intentional effort to create the depth of connection and trust that characterizes family bonds. This process takes time and cannot be rushed, but there are specific ways to nurture these developing relationships.

Creating Emotional Intimacy

Emotional intimacy in chosen family relationships develops through gradual vulnerability and consistent responsiveness. This process involves:

Progressive disclosure: Sharing increasingly personal information as trust develops, allowing both people to demonstrate their ability to handle sensitive information with care.

Responsive listening: Really hearing what the other person is sharing, responding with empathy and understanding, and following up later to show you remember and care about their experiences.

Authentic sharing: Moving beyond surface-level conversation to share your real thoughts, feelings, struggles, and joys. This includes sharing both positive and challenging aspects of your life.

Emotional availability: Being present and engaged during interactions, putting away distractions, and giving your full attention to the relationship.

Validation and support: Offering genuine validation for their experiences and consistent support during difficult times, while also accepting their support for you.

Building Shared History

Chosen family bonds are strengthened by creating shared experiences and memories that become part of your collective story. Some potential shared experiences are:

Regular rituals: Establishing ongoing traditions like weekly phone calls, monthly dinners, annual trips, or holiday celebrations that create predictable connection points.

Shared adventures: Engaging in new experiences together, travel, classes, hobbies, or challenges, that create memories and deepen your bond.

Supporting each other through milestones: Being present for important life events, both joyful and challenging, and creating new traditions around celebrating achievements and supporting each other through difficulties.

Creating inside jokes and shared language: Developing the kind of intimate communication that comes from shared experiences and a deep understanding of each other.

Navigating Conflict Constructively

Healthy chosen family relationships require the ability to work through disagreements and conflicts without damaging the underlying bond. Some healthy ways to navigate conflict are:

Direct communication: Addressing issues openly and honestly rather than letting resentments build or engaging in passive-aggressive behavior.

Taking responsibility: Owning your mistakes, apologizing genuinely when appropriate, and being willing to make changes when you've caused harm.

Assuming positive intent: Giving each other the benefit of the doubt and approaching conflicts with curiosity about understanding each other rather than winning or being right.

Repairing ruptures: When conflicts or misunderstandings occur, actively work to repair the relationship and restore trust and connection.

Balancing Individual Needs and Relationship Needs

Healthy chosen family relationships respect both individual autonomy and relationship connection:

Maintaining your authentic self: Continuing to grow and evolve as an individual while staying connected to your chosen family members.

Respecting different life paths: Supporting each other's choices even when they're different from what you would choose, and maintaining connection despite different life circumstances.

Balancing togetherness and separateness: Enjoying time together while also maintaining your individual friendships, interests, and independence.

Communicating changing needs: Being honest about how your needs in the relationship might change over time and negotiating adjustments that work for both people.

Creating New Traditions and Rituals

One of the joys of a chosen family is the opportunity to create new traditions that reflect your actual values and preferences rather than inherited patterns that may not serve you. These traditions become important markers of your chosen family identity and create shared meaning and connection.

Holiday and Celebration Traditions

Friendsgiving: Creating Thanksgiving celebrations with chosen family that focus on gratitude, connection, and favorite foods rather than obligatory gatherings with difficult relatives.

Chosen family holidays: Establishing your own holiday celebrations that might combine elements from different cultural traditions, focus on values that matter to you, or create entirely new ways of marking important times of year.

Birthday celebrations: Creating meaningful ways to celebrate each other's birthdays that reflect your actual preferences rather than generic celebrations.

Achievement celebrations: Establishing traditions around celebrating each other's successes, milestones, and personal growth in ways that feel authentic and supportive.

Seasonal celebrations: Marking changes of seasons, solstices, or other natural cycles in ways that connect you to each other and to larger rhythms of life.

Regular Connection Rituals

Weekly check-ins: Establishing regular phone calls, video chats, or in-person meetings that maintain connection regardless of busy schedules or life changes.

Monthly gatherings: Creating ongoing traditions like potluck dinners, game nights, movie nights, or other regular activities that bring your chosen family together.

Annual traditions: Planning yearly activities like trips, retreats, or special events that everyone looks forward to and that strengthen your bonds over time.

Support rituals: Developing specific ways of showing up for each other during difficult times, such as bringing meals during illness, helping with moves, or providing childcare during emergencies.

Milestone and Transition Rituals

Coming of age celebrations: Creating meaningful ways to mark important life transitions like graduations, new jobs, relationship milestones, or personal growth achievements.

Healing celebrations: Acknowledging progress in therapy, recovery, or healing from trauma with your chosen family's support and recognition.

New beginning rituals: Marking fresh starts like moving to new cities, starting new careers, or beginning new life phases with a chosen family celebration and blessing.

169

Memorial and grief rituals: Supporting each other through losses and creating meaningful ways to honor deceased loved ones or grieve other types of losses together.

Dealing with Challenges in Chosen Family Relationships

Like all deep relationships, chosen family bonds will face challenges and difficulties. Having skills for navigating these challenges can help strengthen rather than damage your relationships.

When Life Circumstances Change

Geographic distance: Maintaining connection when chosen family members move away, through regular communication, visits when possible, and creative ways of staying involved in each other's lives.

Relationship changes: Navigating when chosen family members get married, have children, or enter new relationships that change the dynamics of your connection.

Career or life phase transitions: Supporting each other through major life changes like career shifts, retirement, health challenges, or other transitions that affect the time and energy available for relationships.

Different life priorities: Respecting when chosen family members need to focus on different priorities while maintaining the underlying bond and connection.

Navigating Disappointments

Unmet expectations: Learning to handle times when chosen family members fall short of your hopes, and recognizing the difference between temporary struggles and true incompatibility.

Communication breakdowns: Repairing relationships after misunderstandings, miscommunications, or conflicts that temporarily damage trust or connection.

Boundary violations: Addressing times when chosen family members cross your boundaries, while determining whether these violations can be repaired or represent deeper incompatibility.

Growth in different directions: Navigating periods when you and chosen family members are growing or changing in ways that create temporary distance or tension.

Maintaining Balance

Avoiding codependency: Maintaining healthy interdependence rather than becoming overly dependent on chosen family members for all your emotional needs.

Respecting individual autonomy: Supporting each other's individual growth and choices even when they're difficult or create temporary distance in the relationship.

Managing group dynamics: When your chosen family includes multiple people, navigating group dynamics, different personalities, and potential conflicts between members.

Integrating romantic relationships: Helping chosen family members welcome new romantic partners while maintaining the core chosen family bonds.

The Ongoing Evolution of Chosen Family

Chosen family relationships are living, evolving connections that change over time as people grow, circumstances shift, and life unfolds. Understanding this evolution can help you maintain realistic expectations and appreciate these relationships for what they offer in each season.

Different Seasons of Connection

Intense bonding phases: Periods when you're particularly close and connected, often during times of mutual need, shared experiences, or life transitions.

Stable maintenance phases: Times when the relationship continues steadily without dramatic intensity, characterized by consistent but perhaps less frequent connection.

Growth and change phases: Periods when one or both people are experiencing significant personal growth that may temporarily affect the relationship dynamics.

Reunion and rediscovery phases: Times when you reconnect more deeply after periods of distance, often leading to renewed appreciation and deeper understanding.

Allowing Natural Evolution

Accepting changing needs: Recognizing that your needs for connection and support may change over time, and that healthy relationships can adapt to these changes.

Welcoming new members: Embracing the possibility of new people entering your chosen family circle, while cherishing those who are already part of it.

Grieving endings: When chosen family relationships end due to irreconcilable differences or life circumstances, allow yourself to grieve these losses while appreciating what the relationships gave you.

Celebrating longevity: Recognizing and celebrating chosen family relationships that endure over many years, acknowledging the precious gift of long-term chosen family bonds.

Building Legacy and Continuity

As chosen family relationships mature, they often develop their own sense of legacy and continuity.

Sharing wisdom: Passing on insights, experiences, and wisdom gained through your chosen family relationships to newer members or younger people.

Creating documentation: Keeping photos, stories, and memories that capture the history and evolution of your chosen family relationships.

Establishing traditions: Developing enduring traditions that can be passed on to future generations or new chosen family members.

Modeling healthy relationships: Demonstrating through your chosen family relationships what healthy, supportive family dynamics can look like.

Reflection: Building Your Chosen Family Map and Plan

Use this comprehensive exercise to assess your current chosen family, identify opportunities for growth, and create an intentional plan for building the supportive relationships you desire.

Current Chosen Family Assessment

Existing Chosen Family Members:

For each person you consider chosen family, reflect on:

Name: _____

- How long have you known each other? _____
- What makes them chosen family vs. "just" friends? _____
- What role do they play in your life? (mentor, sibling-friend, chosen parent, etc.) _____
- How do they support your growth and healing? _____
- What traditions or rituals do you share? _____
- What challenges, if any, exist in this relationship? _____

Chosen Family Strengths:

- What needs does your current chosen family meet well?
- What types of support do you reliably receive?
- What traditions or connections bring you the most joy?
- Which relationships feel most stable and nurturing?

Chosen Family Gaps:

- What types of support or connection are missing?
- Are there certain life areas where you lack chosen family support?

- What kinds of people or relationships would enhance your chosen family?
- Are there specific needs that aren't being met?

Potential Chosen Family Assessment

People in Your Life with Chosen Family Potential:

For each person who might become a closer chosen family member:

Name: _____

- What draws you to them as a potential chosen family member?
- What chosen family qualities do they demonstrate?
- What would need to develop for them to become a chosen family member?
- What steps could you take to deepen this relationship?

Red Flags to Monitor:

- Are there people in your life who seem appealing but show concerning patterns?
- What specific red flags have you noticed?
- How will you maintain appropriate boundaries with these individuals?

Relationship Development Plan

Deepening Existing Relationships:

Choose 2-3 existing relationships you'd like to deepen:

Relationship 1: _____

- Specific ways you could increase emotional intimacy: _____
- Traditions or rituals you already share:_____
- New traditions or rituals you could establish: _____
- How you could better support their growth: _____
- Conversations you'd like to have to deepen connection: _____

Relationship 2: _____

- Specific ways you could increase emotional intimacy: _____
- Traditions or rituals you already share:_____
- New traditions or rituals you could establish: _____
- How you could better support their growth: _____

- Conversations you'd like to have to deepen connection: _____

Building New Connections:

Where I'm most likely to meet potential chosen family members:

- Professional/work environments: _____
- Hobby or interest groups: _____
- Volunteer organizations: _____
- Spiritual or philosophical communities: _____
- Support groups or therapy groups: _____
- Classes or learning environments: _____
- Online communities: _____

Qualities I want to prioritize in new chosen family relationships:

1.
2.
3.
4.
5.

Tradition and Ritual Planning

Existing Traditions to Maintain or Enhance:

- Which current traditions with your chosen family bring you the most joy?
- How could you enhance or deepen these existing traditions?
- What new elements could you add to current celebrations?

New Traditions You'd Like to Create:

Holiday Traditions:

- How do you want to celebrate major holidays with your chosen family?
- What new holiday traditions reflect your values and preferences?
- How can you create inclusive celebrations that welcome different backgrounds?

Regular Connection Rituals:

- What regular check-ins or gatherings would strengthen your chosen family bonds?
- How often do you want to connect with different chosen family members?

- What formats work best for maintaining connection?

Milestone Celebrations:

- How do you want to celebrate chosen family members' achievements?
- What rituals could mark important life transitions?
- How can you create meaningful ways to support each other through challenges?

Seasonal or Annual Traditions:

- What yearly activities would you like to establish with your chosen family?
- Are there seasonal celebrations that resonate with your values?
- What shared experiences would create lasting memories?

Communication and Conflict Resolution Plan

Communication Strategies:

- In what ways can you allow yourself to share more openly with chosen family members over time?
- What topics do you want to be able to discuss openly?
- How will you ask for support when you need it?
- What boundaries do you need to maintain even with your chosen family?

Conflict Resolution Approach:

- How will you address disagreements or conflicts constructively?
- What repair strategies will you use when relationships are strained?
- How will you take responsibility for your mistakes?
- What support will you seek when chosen family conflicts feel overwhelming?

Support System Development

Types of Support You Want to Give and Receive:

Emotional Support:

- How do you best provide emotional support to others?
- What kind of emotional support do you most need?
- How will you communicate your emotional needs clearly?

Practical Support:

- What practical help can you offer chosen family members?
- What practical support do you need from others?

- How will you ask for help when you need it?

Growth Support:

- How do you want to support chosen family members' personal growth?
- What kind of growth support do you want from others?
- How will you celebrate each other's progress and achievements?

Crisis Support:

- What will you do when chosen family members face crises?
- Who can you count on during your own crisis situations?
- How will you communicate about crisis support needs and boundaries?

Integration with Life Circumstances

Balancing Chosen Family with Other Relationships:

- How will you integrate your chosen family with romantic relationships?
- What boundaries do you need around biological family interactions?
- How will you balance chosen family time with other friendships?
- What happens if chosen family members don't get along with each other?

Adapting to Life Changes:

- How will you maintain chosen family connections during major life transitions?
- What happens when you or chosen family members move away?
- How will you adapt relationships when life priorities change?
- What happens when chosen family members have children or major relationship changes?

Timeline and Goals

Six-Month Goals:

- Specific steps I'll take to deepen existing chosen family relationships: _____

- New connections I'll try to develop: _____
- Traditions or rituals I'll establish: _____
- Personal growth I'll focus on to be a better chosen family member: _____

One-Year Goals:

- How I want my chosen family circle to look: _____
- Major traditions or celebrations I want to establish: _____
- Relationship skills I want to develop: _____
- Support systems I want to have in place: _____

Five-Year Vision:

- What kind of chosen family legacy do I want to create?
- How do I want to be remembered as a chosen family member?
- What traditions do I hope will continue long-term?
- How do I want my chosen family to evolve as we all grow and change?

Gratitude and Appreciation

Current Gratitude:

- What am I most grateful for about my existing chosen family?
- How have chosen family relationships contributed to my healing and growth?
- What moments or experiences with your chosen family bring you the most joy?

Appreciation Expression:

- How will I regularly express appreciation to chosen family members?
- What specific things do I want to acknowledge about their support?
- How will I celebrate the gift of chosen family in my life?

Remember, building your chosen family is a gradual process that unfolds over time. Not every person you meet will become part of your chosen family, and that's perfectly normal. The goal is to be open to deep connections while maintaining healthy boundaries, to invest in relationships that genuinely nourish you, and to create the kinds of family bonds that support your authentic self and your continued growth and healing.

Your chosen family is one of the greatest gifts you can give yourself—and one of the greatest gifts you can be to others who need the experience of healthy, loving family relationships. Trust the process, stay open to connection, and remember that the family you choose can be every bit as meaningful and life-giving as the family you were born into, and often more so.

Chapter 14: Healing and Moving Forward

After making the difficult decision to cut ties with toxic family members and establishing the boundaries necessary to protect your well-being, you face a new challenge: how to heal from the years of damage and create a life that reflects your authentic self rather than your survival mechanisms. This chapter isn't about getting over your experiences or pretending they didn't happen. It's about transforming your relationship with your past so that it becomes a source of wisdom and strength rather than ongoing pain.

Healing from toxic family relationships is both similar to and different from healing from other types of trauma. It's similar in that it requires processing grief, developing new neural pathways, and learning to trust yourself and others again. It's different because family trauma often involves the people who were supposed to provide your foundation of safety and love, meaning the healing process involves not just recovering from harm but learning fundamental skills about relationships, self-worth, and emotional regulation that many people develop naturally in healthy families.

This chapter will guide you through the various aspects of healing: understanding what healing actually looks like, developing a relationship with your inner child, learning to regulate your emotions, building self-worth from the inside out, and creating a vision for your life that's based on your authentic desires rather than reactive patterns. Most importantly, we'll explore how your painful experiences can become a source of empowerment and wisdom that allows you to live with greater compassion, resilience, and authenticity.

What Healing Actually Looks Like

One of the hardest parts of being an adult with attachment trauma is looking back on your life and wondering what could have been. But if we don't address the past properly, we will assume the future will look just like the past to us. We will filter our hopes through a lens of trepidation and dread, shaped by what we have already gone through.

Many people have unrealistic expectations about what healing from family trauma should look like. They imagine it as a clear-cut process that ends with complete resolution, total forgiveness, and the absence of any emotional response to past hurts. This version of healing sets people up for disappointment and can make them feel like they're failing when the reality of healing is messier, more complex, and more gradual than this fantasy suggests.

Healing Is Not Forgetting

Healing doesn't mean you forget what happened to you or that you stop having any emotional response to your experiences. Your memories are part of your story, and attempting to erase them would actually impede healing rather than promote it. Instead, healing means developing a different relationship with your memories, one where they inform and strengthen you rather than controlling and limiting you.

When you've healed from family trauma, you can remember difficult experiences without being overwhelmed by them. You can acknowledge what happened without being consumed by anger or stuck in victim narratives. You can use your experiences as information about what you need and want in relationships without assuming everyone will hurt you in the same ways.

This doesn't mean your memories become pleasant or that you feel grateful for traumatic experiences. It means you develop the capacity to hold your memories with compassion for yourself while no longer being controlled by the fear, shame, or rage they once triggered.

Healing Is a Winding Path

The healing process involves cycles, setbacks, breakthroughs, and periods of integration. You might feel like you've worked through an issue only to have it resurface months later in a different form or triggered by a new situation. This isn't failure; it's the natural process of healing complex trauma that has affected multiple areas of your development.

Some days you'll feel strong, confident, and grateful for your growth. Other days, you might feel sad, angry, or discouraged about your progress. Both experiences are part of healing. The goal isn't to eliminate difficult emotions but to develop the capacity to feel them without being overwhelmed or making decisions from reactive states.

Think of healing like peeling an onion—each layer you work through reveals another layer underneath. This can feel frustrating, but it's also evidence that you're going deeper into authentic healing rather than just managing surface symptoms.

Healing Is Integration, Not Perfection

It's okay to not know everything about yourself yet. This is all part of healing from identity loss. Healing from identity loss is a slow process, but you'll come out stronger, more dignified, and more assertive than ever before.

Healthy people aren't people who never struggle or never have difficult emotions. They're people who have learned to work with their struggles constructively rather than being controlled by them. Healing means integrating all parts of your experience, the painful and the joyful, the wounded and the resilient, into a coherent sense of self that can navigate life's challenges with wisdom and self-compassion.

Integration involves acknowledging your vulnerabilities without being defined by them, using your painful experiences as sources of empathy and wisdom, and developing the ability to be present with difficult emotions without being overwhelmed by them. It means accepting that you're a complex human being with both strengths and areas for continued growth.

Signs of Healing Progress

While healing isn't a neat, step-by-step process, there are signs that indicate you're moving in a healthy direction. Some of the signs are:

Increased emotional regulation: You experience intense emotions less frequently and recover from them more quickly. When you do feel overwhelmed, you have tools and strategies that help you regain balance.

Better boundary setting: You can identify your limits more clearly and communicate them more effectively. You're less likely to overextend yourself or accept treatment that doesn't align with your values.

Improved relationships: Your relationships become more authentic and reciprocal. You're able to form deeper connections with people who treat you well and recognize red flags more quickly in unhealthy relationships.

Greater self-compassion: You treat yourself with kindness and understanding rather than harsh criticism. You can acknowledge your mistakes and struggles without spiraling into shame or self-attack.

Increased resilience: While challenges still affect you, you bounce back more quickly and use difficulties as opportunities for growth rather than evidence of your inadequacy.

Clarity about values and goals: You have a clearer sense of what matters to you and what you want your life to look like, based on your authentic preferences rather than reactions to your past.

Reduced reactivity: You're less likely to be triggered by reminders of past trauma or to make important decisions from emotional reactivity. You can pause, reflect, and choose your responses more consciously.

Developing a Relationship with Your Inner Child

Growing up in narcissistic, toxic, and scapegoating dynamics meant they were actively trained to sideline themselves. They were expected to push their needs to the side, swallow their feelings, and dampen their pain. They were conditioned to deny their perceptions, twist their reality, and plaster on a mask to please and placate others. But it wasn't just their pain they ignored and contorted, it was their joy as well.

One of the most powerful aspects of healing from family trauma involves developing a conscious, nurturing relationship with your inner child, the part of you that holds your earliest wounds, unmet needs, and authentic essence. This isn't just a therapeutic metaphor; it's a practical way of healing the developmental disruptions that occurred during your childhood and reclaiming the parts of yourself that may have gone underground for survival.

Understanding Your Inner Child

Your inner child represents the emotional, intuitive, creative, and vulnerable aspects of yourself that were shaped by your early experiences. In healthy families, children learn that their emotions are valid, their needs matter, and they're worthy of love and protection. In toxic families, children often learn the opposite: that their feelings are wrong, their needs are burdensome, and they must earn love through performance or compliance.

The strategies your inner child developed to survive a toxic family environment were intelligent adaptations to abnormal circumstances. However, these same strategies may now interfere with your ability to form healthy relationships, pursue your authentic desires, or feel deserving of good things in your life.

Common inner child wounds from toxic family dynamics include:

- *Abandonment wounds*: Fear that people will leave you if you're not perfect or if you have needs that feel inconvenient to others.

- *Rejection wounds*: Deep fear that your authentic self is somehow fundamentally unacceptable or unlovable.

- *Betrayal wounds*: Difficulty trusting others because the people who were supposed to protect you instead caused harm.

- *Neglect wounds*: Feeling invisible, unimportant, or like your needs don't matter because they were consistently ignored or minimized.

- *Engulfment wounds*: Fear of losing yourself in relationships because your boundaries weren't respected and your individual identity wasn't encouraged.

Recognizing Your Inner Child's Voice

Your inner child often communicates through:

Emotional reactions that feel disproportionate: When you have strong emotional responses that seem bigger than the current situation warrants, your inner child may be responding to past experiences that the current situation has triggered.

Body sensations and intuitive responses: Your inner child often speaks through gut feelings, physical sensations, or sudden energy shifts that provide important information about safety and well-being.

Creative impulses and spontaneous joy: Moments when you feel drawn to creative expression, play, or activities that bring pure delight often come from your inner child.

Sudden fears or anxieties: Unexplained fears or anxieties often stem from your inner child's memories of times when you weren't safe or protected.

Longing for care and nurturing: Desires to be comforted, held, or cared for by others often represent your inner child's unmet needs for safety and love.

Reparenting Yourself

Reparenting involves consciously providing yourself with the nurturing, guidance, and protection that you needed but didn't receive in childhood. This isn't about blaming your parents or trying to redo the past—it's about taking responsibility for meeting your own emotional needs in healthy ways as an adult.

Emotional nurturing: Learning to comfort yourself during difficult times, validate your own feelings, and speak to yourself with the kindness you would show a beloved child. This might involve holding yourself while you cry, speaking soothing words to yourself, or creating comfort routines that help you feel safe.

Setting protective boundaries: Advocating for yourself in situations where others might take advantage of you, and removing yourself from relationships or situations that are harmful to your well-being. Your adult self learns to be the protective parent your inner child needs.

Providing structure and guidance: Creating healthy routines, making decisions that support your long-term well-being even when they're difficult in the moment, and developing life skills that help you function effectively as an adult.

Encouraging growth and exploration: Supporting your own interests, dreams, and creative expressions without judgment or pressure to be perfect. This means giving yourself permission to try new things, make mistakes, and pursue activities simply because they bring you joy.

Meeting practical needs: Ensuring you have adequate food, rest, healthcare, and other basic necessities, and not neglecting your physical well-being even during stressful times. Many people from toxic families learned to ignore their physical needs, and reparenting involves learning to prioritize their health and comfort.

Inner Child Healing Practices

Journaling with your inner child: Write with your non-dominant hand to access childlike expression, or engage in written dialogues between your adult self and your inner child about their needs, fears, and desires.

Creative expression: Engage in creative activities that your inner child enjoys without pressure to produce anything valuable or impressive. The goal is process, not product.

Play and joy: Deliberately engage in activities that bring you pure joy and playfulness, reconnecting with the parts of yourself that may have been suppressed during survival-focused childhood years.

Visualization and imagery: Use guided meditations or visualizations where you meet and comfort your inner child, providing them with the safety and love they need.

Photo work: Look at childhood photos of yourself with compassion and love, speaking to that child with the kindness they deserved to receive. Many people find it helpful to keep a childhood photo where they can see it and practice sending love to that younger version of themselves.

Inner child letters: Write letters to your inner child expressing love, validation, and protection. You can also write letters from your inner child to your adult self, expressing their needs and feelings.

Integrating Your Inner Child

The goal isn't to become childlike but to integrate the healthy aspects of your inner child with your adult wisdom and capabilities. This integration allows you to:

- Trust your intuitive responses to people and situations
- Express your authentic emotions without shame
- Pursue activities and relationships that bring you genuine joy
- Set boundaries based on your actual feelings rather than what you think you should do
- Access creativity and spontaneity in your daily life
- Feel deserving of love, care, and good things

When your inner child feels heard, loved, and protected by your adult self, they become a source of vitality, creativity, and authentic connection rather than a source of overwhelming emotions or self-sabotaging behaviors.

Learning Emotional Regulation

This internalized sense of helplessness can contribute further to a reduced sense of self and reinforce the toxic dynamics of the relationship. Indeed, it is fruitless to reason with a narcissistic abuser, and probably safer to just stop trying after a while. You're just a glutton for punishment if you provoke them. The problem is that this helpless attitude tends to generalize towards all of life. This is completely normal, understandable, and predictable. It happens to anyone who has lived through the pain of a narcissistic, abusive relationship.

Many people from toxic families never learned healthy emotional regulation skills because their emotions were either ignored, punished, or used against them. As a result, they may struggle with feeling overwhelmed by emotions, numbing out emotionally, or swinging between emotional extremes without a middle ground.

Understanding Emotional Dysregulation

Emotional dysregulation can manifest in various ways.

Overwhelming emotions: Feeling flooded by emotions that seem disproportionate to the situation or that last much longer than feels appropriate.

Emotional numbing: Feeling disconnected from your emotions or unable to access feelings even when they would be appropriate and helpful.

Rapid emotional swings: Moving quickly between different emotional states without warning or apparent reason.

Difficulty identifying emotions: Struggling to name what you're feeling or understand why you're having particular emotional responses.

Emotional reactivity: Making important decisions from intense emotional states or having your emotions control your behavior in ways you later regret.

Physical symptoms: Experiencing emotions primarily through physical symptoms like headaches, stomachaches, muscle tension, or fatigue rather than recognizing them as emotions.

The Window of Tolerance

Healthy emotional regulation involves learning to stay within your window of tolerance, the zone where you can experience emotions without becoming overwhelmed or shutting down. When you're outside this window, you're either in hyperarousal (feeling overwhelmed, anxious, angry, or panicked) or hypoarousal (feeling numb, disconnected, depressed, or shut down).

People from toxic families often have narrow windows of tolerance because they learned to either suppress emotions completely or become overwhelmed by them. Healing involves gradually expanding your window of tolerance so you can experience a wider range of emotions without losing your capacity to think clearly and make good decisions.

Building Emotional Regulation Skills

Mindfulness and awareness: Learning to notice your emotional states without immediately reacting to them. This creates space between feeling and action where you can make conscious choices about how to respond. Simple practices like naming your emotions can help create this space.

Somatic awareness: Paying attention to how emotions show up in your body so you can recognize emotional states early and respond before they become overwhelming. Your body often signals emotional changes before your mind recognizes them.

Grounding techniques: Developing strategies for returning to the present moment and your physical body when you feel emotionally activated or dissociated. These might include focusing on your five senses, placing your feet firmly on the ground, or holding a meaningful object.

Self-soothing skills: Learning healthy ways to comfort yourself during difficult emotional states, such as breathing exercises, progressive muscle relaxation, or engaging your senses in calming ways. This is different from avoiding emotions. It's about creating safety so you can experience emotions without being overwhelmed.

Distress tolerance: Building capacity to sit with uncomfortable emotions without immediately trying to escape, change, or fix them. Sometimes emotions just need to be felt and will naturally resolve on their own.

Emotion identification and expression: Developing vocabulary for your emotional experiences and finding healthy ways to express feelings through words, creativity, or physical movement.

Creating Emotional Safety

For many people from toxic families, emotional regulation is difficult because they never felt emotionally safe. Creating internal and external conditions that support emotional safety is crucial for developing regulation skills.

Internal safety: Developing self-compassion, learning to validate your own experiences, and creating internal dialogue that's supportive rather than critical or judgmental.

External safety: Surrounding yourself with people who can handle your emotions without becoming overwhelmed themselves or using your feelings against you.

Environmental safety: Creating physical spaces and routines that feel calming and supportive when you're experiencing difficult emotions.

Relational safety: Building relationships where you can express your authentic feelings without fear of rejection, punishment, or having your emotions used to manipulate you.

Practical Regulation Techniques

The STOP technique: When you notice emotional overwhelm, Stop what you're doing, Take a breath, Observe what's happening in your body and mind, and then Proceed with conscious intention rather than reactive impulse.

Breathing practices: Simple breathing techniques like box breathing (inhale for 4, hold for 4, exhale for 4, hold for 4) can quickly activate your parasympathetic nervous system and help regulate emotions.

Temperature regulation: Using temperature changes (cold water on your face, ice cubes, warm bath) can quickly shift your emotional state when you're feeling overwhelmed.

Movement and exercise: Physical movement helps process emotional energy and can be particularly effective for managing anger, anxiety, or restless energy.

Creative expression: Drawing, writing, singing, or other creative activities can help you express and process emotions that are difficult to put into words.

Building Authentic Self-Worth

Reclaiming your identity means prioritizing your well-being. This might mean limiting contact with toxic individuals, saying no to things that don't align with your healing, or creating space for self-care. Boundaries help you regain control over your life.

One of the deepest wounds from toxic family relationships is damage to your sense of inherent worth and value. When the people who were supposed to love you unconditionally instead made their love conditional on your performance, compliance, or ability to meet their needs, you may have internalized the belief that you must earn your worth rather than possessing it simply by being human.

Understanding Conditional vs. Unconditional Worth

In toxic families, worth is often conditional:

- You're valuable when you achieve or perform well
- You're lovable when you make others happy or comfortable
- You matter when you're useful or needed
- You deserve good things when you've been "good enough"

Healthy self-worth, in contrast, is unconditional:

- You have value simply because you exist
- You're worthy of love and respect regardless of your achievements
- Your needs and feelings matter because you're human
- You deserve good things in your life, not because you've earned them, but because all humans deserve safety, love, and opportunities for happiness

Recognizing Internalized Messages

The first step in building authentic self-worth is recognizing the specific messages about worth and value that you internalized from your family experiences.

Perfectionism: The belief that you must be perfect to be acceptable, and that any mistakes or failures reflect fundamental flaws in your character.

People-pleasing: The assumption that your worth depends on making others happy, comfortable, or pleased with you, even at the expense of your own needs and values.

Achievement addiction: The need to constantly accomplish things or reach new goals to feel valuable, with your sense of worth tied to external recognition or success.

Self-sacrifice: The belief that your needs and desires are less important than others', and that love requires you to consistently put others first.

Hyperresponsibility: Taking responsibility for things that aren't actually your responsibility, including other people's emotions, choices, and well-being.

Shame-based identity: Believing that there's something fundamentally wrong or bad about you that makes you unworthy of good treatment or genuine love.

Developing Intrinsic Self-Worth

Building authentic self-worth involves shifting from external validation to internal validation and developing a relationship with yourself based on compassion rather than criticism.

Self-compassion practices: Learning to treat yourself with the same kindness you would show a good friend, especially during difficult times or when you make mistakes. This includes speaking to yourself kindly, acknowledging your struggles without judgment, and recognizing that suffering and imperfection are part of the human experience.

Values-based living: Making decisions based on your authentic values rather than what you think will make others approve of you or what you think you should do. This requires first identifying what you actually value versus what you were taught to value.

Celebrating small wins: Acknowledging your progress and efforts rather than only recognizing major achievements or perfect outcomes. This might mean celebrating showing up to a difficult conversation, setting a boundary, or simply getting through a challenging day.

Internal validation: Learning to validate your own experiences, feelings, and perceptions rather than constantly seeking confirmation from others. This includes trusting your own judgment about what you've experienced and what you need.

Boundary setting: Recognizing that protecting your well-being and saying no to things that don't serve you are acts of self-respect rather than selfishness.

Accepting your humanity: Embracing the fact that you're a complex human being with both strengths and areas for growth, and that this complexity is normal and acceptable.

Challenging the Inner Critic

For those still waiting for an external confirmation of their pain, the hardest but most liberating realization is this: You don't need their permission to tell your story. You don't need their validation to know it was real. You don't need a courtroom to reclaim your truth.

Most people from toxic families have developed harsh inner critics that echo the judgmental voices they heard growing up. Learning to recognize and challenge this inner critic is essential for building healthy self-worth.

Identify the critic's voice: Notice when your internal dialogue becomes harsh, judgmental, or demeaning. Often, this voice sounds like specific family members or uses language that echoes childhood criticism.

Question the critic's authority: Ask yourself whether the critical voice is based on truth or on old messages that may not be accurate or helpful. Would you speak to a good friend the way your inner critic speaks to you?

Develop a compassionate inner voice: Consciously practice speaking to yourself with kindness, understanding, and encouragement. This takes practice, but over time, you can develop an internal voice that supports rather than undermines you.

Challenge perfectionist standards: Recognize when you're holding yourself to impossible standards and practice accepting "good enough" as truly good enough.

Reframe self-criticism: Instead of "I'm terrible at this," try "I'm learning and improving." Instead of "I always mess things up," try "I made a mistake and I can learn from it."

Practical Self-Worth Building Exercises

Daily affirmations: Develop personal affirmations that counter specific negative beliefs you internalized. These should be statements you can believe, even if you don't feel them strongly yet.

Accomplishment lists: Regularly write down things you've accomplished, including small everyday victories like having a difficult conversation or taking care of your health.

Gratitude for yourself: Practice being grateful for your own qualities, efforts, and growth, not just for external things or other people.

Self-care as self-respect: Engage in activities that nurture your physical, emotional, and spiritual well-being, recognizing these as expressions of your inherent worth.

Boundary celebration: Acknowledge and celebrate moments when you set healthy boundaries, recognizing these as acts of self-respect rather than selfishness.

Creating a Vision for Your Authentic Life

Your trauma is part of your story, but it doesn't have to be your entire identity. Instead of saying, "I am broken," try reframing it: "I have been through something difficult, but I am healing." Recognizing what you've been through while shifting your narrative empowers you to move forward.

As you heal from family trauma and develop a stronger sense of self, you can begin creating a vision for your life that's based on your authentic desires rather than reactions to your past or attempts to prove your worth. This vision serves as a North Star that guides your decisions and helps you build a life that truly reflects who you are becoming.

Distinguishing Between Reactive and Authentic Goals

Many people from toxic families initially set goals that are reactions to their past rather than expressions of their authentic selves.

Reactive goals might include:

- Achieving success primarily to prove your worth or show your family they were wrong about you

- Choosing careers or relationships that are the opposite of what your family would approve of

- Accumulating wealth or status symbols to compensate for feeling worthless

- Avoiding anything that reminds you of your family, even if it might actually bring you joy

- Making decisions primarily based on what will make you feel safe rather than what will help you thrive

Authentic goals emerge from:

- Your genuine interests, values, and passions

- A desire to contribute meaningfully to the world in ways that align with your strengths

- Natural curiosity and excitement about particular activities or experiences

- A sense of what would bring you deep satisfaction rather than just external validation

- Values-based decision making that considers both your well-being and your positive impact on others

Exploring Your Authentic Desires

After years of survival-focused living, you might not immediately know what you authentically want. This exploration process requires patience and self-compassion. Ways to help you figure out what you authentically want.

Pay attention to what energizes you: Notice activities, conversations, and experiences that make you feel alive and engaged rather than drained or obligated.

Identify your natural strengths: Recognize things you do well naturally, not just skills you've developed to meet others' expectations or survive difficult circumstances.

Explore childhood dreams: Consider interests or dreams you had before they were discouraged or before survival became your primary focus. What did you love to do before you learned to focus on pleasing others?

Notice what makes you lose track of time: Pay attention to activities where you become so absorbed that you forget about time passing or external concerns.

Consider your values: Reflect on what principles and values truly matter to you, beyond what you think you should value based on family or cultural expectations.

Imagine unlimited resources: If you had unlimited time, money, and support, what would you want to do with your life? This exercise can help you uncover your true desires, even ones that may feel out of reach, and use them to guide smaller, doable steps forward.

Listen to your body: Your body often knows what you need and want before your mind does. Pay attention to what makes you feel energized versus drained, what environments feel nourishing versus depleting.

Building a Life Around Your Authentic Self

Creating an authentic life often involves making significant changes in various areas.

Career and work: Pursuing work that aligns with your values and uses your natural strengths, rather than just providing financial security or external validation. This might mean changing careers, starting a business, or finding ways to bring more meaning to your current work.

Relationships: Prioritizing relationships that support your authentic self and allow you to be genuine, rather than relationships that require you to perform or hide parts of yourself. This includes both deepening healthy relationships and distancing from relationships that drain you.

Living environment: Creating physical spaces that reflect your actual preferences and support your well-being, rather than what you think you should want or what others expect. This might involve redecorating, moving, or simply organizing your space in ways that feel nurturing.

Daily routines: Developing rhythms and practices that support your physical, emotional, and spiritual well-being rather than just maintaining productivity or meeting others' expectations.

Recreation and hobbies: Engaging in activities that bring you genuine joy and fulfillment, not just activities that make you look good or productive to others.

Social and community involvement: Participating in communities and causes that align with your values and allow you to contribute in meaningful ways.

Navigating the Transition

Moving from survival-focused living to authentic living is often challenging and can trigger anxiety, guilt, or fear.

Start small: Make gradual changes rather than trying to transform your entire life at once. Small, consistent steps toward authenticity are more sustainable than dramatic overhauls.

Expect resistance: Your nervous system and habitual patterns may resist changes, even positive ones. This resistance is normal and doesn't mean you're making wrong choices.

Prepare for others' reactions: Some people in your life may not understand or support your changes, especially if they benefited from your previous patterns of people-pleasing or self-sacrifice. They may even get angry about your changes.

Build support: Surround yourself with people who encourage your authentic self-expression and can provide encouragement during challenging transitions.

Practice self-compassion: Be patient with yourself during this process and remember that building an authentic life is a lifelong journey, not a destination you reach once and for all.

Celebrate progress: Acknowledge and celebrate each step you take toward authentic living, even if progress feels slow or incomplete.

Post-Traumatic Growth and Finding Meaning

PTSD can now be effectively and permanently healed with the right support. We all have an innate drive towards healing, growth, connection, and aliveness. Nobody can do it for you, and you can't do it alone. I'm here to help, you're worth it, and you can do it.

While trauma is never something to be grateful for, many people who heal from family trauma experience what psychologists call "post-traumatic growth", which are positive changes that emerge from working through difficult experiences. This doesn't mean that trauma is good or necessary, but rather that humans have a remarkable capacity to find meaning and develop strength through adversity.

Areas of Post-Traumatic Growth

Enhanced relationships: Many trauma survivors develop a deeper capacity for authentic intimacy, stronger boundaries, and a better ability to recognize healthy vs. unhealthy relationship patterns. Having experienced the pain of toxic relationships, they become skilled at identifying and creating healthier connections.

Increased personal strength: Going through the healing process often reveals inner resources and resilience you didn't know you possessed. Many people discover they're stronger and more capable than they ever imagined.

Greater appreciation for life: Having experienced significant pain can increase appreciation for joy, beauty, connection, and simple pleasures. Many trauma survivors report feeling more grateful for small positive experiences than they did before their healing journey.

Spiritual development: Many people develop or deepen spiritual beliefs and practices as part of their healing journey. This might involve traditional religious practices or more personal spiritual explorations about meaning and purpose.

Clearer life priorities: Trauma often clarifies what truly matters, leading to more intentional choices about how to spend time and energy. Many people report being less concerned with superficial matters and more focused on meaningful relationships and activities.

Increased empathy and compassion: Personal experience with suffering often increases the capacity to understand and support others who are struggling. This enhanced empathy can become a source of deep connection and meaningful contribution to others' lives.

Finding Meaning in Your Experience

Finding meaning doesn't require being grateful for trauma or minimizing its impact. Instead, it involves recognizing how your experiences have shaped you in ways that can benefit both you and others.

Using your experience to help others: Many trauma survivors find purpose in supporting others who are going through similar experiences, whether through formal helping professions, volunteer work, or simply being a source of understanding and hope for friends and family members.

Breaking generational cycles: By healing your own trauma, you prevent passing traumatic patterns to future generations, creating a legacy of healing rather than harm. This might be one of the most significant contributions you can make.

Developing wisdom and insight: Your experiences may have given you insights about human nature, relationships, and resilience that you can use to navigate future challenges more effectively and share with others.

Creating something meaningful: Some people find purpose in creative expression, advocacy work, or other activities that transform their pain into something that benefits the world.

Modeling resilience: Your healing journey can inspire others who may be struggling with their own challenges, showing them that healing and growth are possible even after severe trauma.

Increased compassion for humanity: Understanding the ways that hurt people can hurt others often leads to increased compassion for the human condition and a desire to contribute to reducing suffering in the world.

Avoiding the "Grateful for Trauma" Trap

It's important to distinguish between finding meaning in your healing journey and feeling obligated to be grateful for trauma itself.

- You don't need to be thankful that you were harmed
- You don't need to minimize the impact of your experiences
- You're allowed to wish your childhood had been different
- You can appreciate your growth while still grieving what you lost

Finding meaning is about what you've done with your experiences, not about the experiences themselves being good or necessary. You can honor your resilience and growth while still acknowledging that you deserved better treatment and didn't need to experience trauma to become a strong person.

Practical Steps for Daily Healing

Healing from family trauma happens not just in therapy sessions or dramatic breakthrough moments, but in the accumulation of small, daily choices that support your well-being and authentic self-expression.

Daily Practices for Emotional Regulation

Morning check-ins: Start each day by briefly checking in with yourself about how you're feeling physically, emotionally, and mentally, without judgment or pressure to change anything. This builds self-awareness and helps you prepare for the day ahead.

Breathing practices: Develop simple breathing techniques you can use throughout the day when you notice stress or emotional activation. Even three deep breaths can help regulate your nervous system.

Mindful transitions: Create brief mindful moments between activities to help regulate your nervous system and stay present. This might involve taking a few conscious breaths before entering meetings or pausing to notice your surroundings when you get home.

Evening reflection: End each day by acknowledging what went well, what was challenging, and what you learned about yourself. This helps integrate daily experiences and reinforces your commitment to growth.

Self-Compassion Practices

Loving-kindness meditation: Practice extending kindness and good wishes to yourself, especially during difficult times. Start with phrases like "May I be happy, may I be healthy, may I be at peace."

Self-compassion breaks: When you notice self-criticism, pause and offer yourself the same compassion you would give a good friend. Place your hand on your heart and acknowledge that you're having a difficult moment.

Affirmations: Develop personal affirmations that counter specific negative beliefs you internalized from your family experiences. Make these statements realistic and believable rather than grandiose.

Gratitude for progress: Regularly acknowledge your growth and healing progress, even when it feels slow or incomplete. Keep a record of positive changes you've noticed in yourself.

Boundary Maintenance

Daily boundary check: Notice throughout the day when you feel comfortable vs. uncomfortable in interactions, using these feelings as information about your boundaries.

Practice saying no: Look for small opportunities to practice declining requests or invitations that don't align with your needs or values.

Energy management: Pay attention to what activities and people energize vs. drain you, and make conscious choices about how to spend your time and energy.

Self-advocacy: Practice speaking up for yourself in small, low-stakes situations to build confidence for more significant boundary-setting.

Connection and Community Building

Reach out to supportive people: Make regular contact with people who understand and support your healing journey. This might be as simple as sending a text to check in with a friend.

Express appreciation: Regularly let people know how much their support means to you. This strengthens relationships and creates positive cycles of connection.

Practice vulnerability: Look for appropriate opportunities to share your authentic thoughts and feelings with trusted people. This builds intimacy and helps you practice being genuine.

Offer support to others: Find ways to support others in their own challenges, recognizing that giving and receiving support are both important parts of healthy relationships.

Self-Care as Healing Practice

Physical care: Prioritize basic needs like adequate sleep, nutrition, exercise, and medical care. Many people from toxic families learned to ignore or minimize their physical needs, so attending to your body is an important part of healing.

Emotional care: Create regular practices for processing emotions, whether through journaling, creative expression, therapy, or conversations with trusted friends. Don't let emotions build up until they become overwhelming.

Mental care: Engage in activities that challenge and stimulate your mind in positive ways—reading, learning new skills, solving problems, or engaging in meaningful work that uses your abilities.

Spiritual care: Develop practices that connect you with something larger than yourself, whether through traditional religious practices, time in nature, meditation, or other activities that nurture your sense of meaning and purpose.

Environmental care: Create living and working spaces that feel safe, comfortable, and nurturing. Your environment affects your emotional state, so make choices that support your well-being.

Navigating Setbacks and Difficult Periods

No healing journey is without setbacks, difficult periods, or times when you feel like you're moving backward. Understanding that these challenges are normal parts of the process can help you navigate them with self-compassion rather than self-criticism.

Understanding Healing Setbacks

Trauma anniversaries: Certain times of year, dates, or life circumstances may trigger memories or emotional responses related to past trauma. These anniversary reactions are normal and usually temporary.

New life stresses: Major life changes like job transitions, relationship changes, health challenges, or financial stress can temporarily overwhelm your coping resources and make old patterns resurface.

Growth edges: Sometimes setbacks occur when you're actually making progress but encountering new challenges that require developing new skills or capacities.

Grief waves: As you heal, you may periodically experience waves of grief about what you lost in your family relationships or what you missed in childhood. This grief is part of healing, not a sign of moving backward.

Strategies for Managing Difficult Periods

During challenging times, actively reach out for additional support from friends, family, therapists, or support groups rather than trying to handle everything alone.

Return to basics: Focus on fundamental self-care practices like adequate sleep, nutrition, exercise, and emotional regulation techniques that have helped you before.

Practice self-compassion: Remind yourself that having difficult periods doesn't mean you're failing or that all your progress has been lost. Healing involves ups and downs.

Review your progress: Look back at how far you've come since beginning your healing journey, even if current circumstances make it hard to see your growth.

Adjust expectations: Temporarily lower your expectations for what you can accomplish and focus on just getting through challenging periods without reverting to harmful coping mechanisms.

Seek professional help: If difficult periods persist or interfere significantly with your daily functioning, don't hesitate to seek additional professional support.

Learning from Challenges

Each difficult period in your healing journey offers opportunities for learning and growth.

What triggers are you discovering: New challenges often reveal triggers or vulnerabilities you weren't previously aware of, giving you information about areas that need additional attention.

What coping strategies work: Difficult periods help you discover which coping strategies are most effective for you and which ones need to be strengthened or replaced.

What support do you need: Challenges reveal what kinds of support are most helpful to you and where you might need to build stronger support systems.

What progress you've made: Often, you can see your growth most clearly by noticing how differently you handle similar challenges compared to the past.

Building Resilience for Long-Term Healing

Resilience isn't something you either have or don't have—it's a set of skills and capacities that can be developed over time. Building resilience helps ensure that your healing continues even when you face new challenges or stressful life circumstances.

Core Components of Resilience

Emotional regulation skills: The ability to experience intense emotions without being overwhelmed by them or making important decisions from reactive states.

Cognitive flexibility: The capacity to see situations from multiple perspectives, question negative thought patterns, and adapt your thinking when circumstances change.

Social connection: Strong relationships that provide emotional support, practical help, and a sense of belonging during both good times and challenges.

Meaning-making ability: The skill to find purpose and meaning in your experiences, even difficult ones, and to see challenges as opportunities for growth rather than just threats to endure.

Self-efficacy: Confidence in your ability to handle challenges, solve problems, and create positive change in your life.

Adaptive coping strategies: A toolkit of healthy ways to manage stress, process emotions, and care for yourself during difficult times.

Practices That Build Resilience

Stress inoculation: Gradually exposing yourself to manageable challenges and stressors helps build confidence in your ability to handle difficulties.

Skills development: Continuously learning new skills increases your capacity to handle whatever life brings.

Perspective practices: Regular practices like gratitude, mindfulness, or journaling help you maintain balanced perspectives on your experiences and see the bigger picture.

Physical resilience: Maintaining physical health through exercise, nutrition, and medical care supports your emotional and mental resilience.

Community building: Investing in relationships and community connections creates a support network that can help you weather difficult times.

Recovery practices: Developing effective ways to recover from stress and challenges prevents burnout and maintains your long-term capacity for resilience.

Creating a Personal Healing Plan

As you continue your healing journey, having a personalized plan can help ensure you maintain progress and continue growing even when life gets busy or challenging.

Assessing Your Current Needs

Healing priorities: What aspects of healing feel most important or urgent for you right now? This might include emotional regulation, relationship skills, trauma processing, or building self-worth.

Available resources: What support, time, and financial resources do you have available for your healing work? This helps you create realistic goals and expectations.

Strengths and challenges: What healing work are you already doing well, and where do you need to focus more attention or develop new skills?

Life circumstances: How do your current life circumstances support or challenge your healing efforts?

Components of Your Healing Plan

Professional support: What therapeutic, medical, or other professional support will best serve your healing goals? This might include individual therapy, group therapy, medical care, spiritual counseling, or coaching.

Daily practices: What daily activities will support your ongoing healing and well-being? Include practices for emotional regulation, self-care, connection, and personal growth.

Weekly and monthly activities: What regular activities will support your longer-term healing goals? This might include support group meetings, creative pursuits, volunteer work, or relationship-building activities.

Annual or seasonal goals: What larger healing goals do you want to work toward over the coming year? These might include major life changes, relationship developments, or specific therapeutic goals.

Emergency plan: What will you do during crisis situations or particularly difficult periods? Include contact information for support people and professionals, as well as specific strategies that have helped you in the past.

Regular Review and Adjustment

Your healing plan should be a living document that evolves as you grow and change:

Monthly check-ins: Regularly assess how your healing plan is working and what adjustments might be helpful.

Quarterly reviews: Every few months, take a broader look at your progress and consider whether your goals and strategies need to be updated.

Annual planning: Once a year, reflect on your overall healing journey and set intentions for the coming year.

Flexibility: Remember that your healing plan should serve you, not the other way around. Be willing to adjust your plan when circumstances change or when you discover new needs or interests.

Reflection: Creating Your Personal Healing Plan

Use this comprehensive exercise to assess your current healing needs and create a personalized plan for ongoing growth and recovery.

Current Healing Assessment

Areas of Strength:

- What aspects of healing am I doing well with?
- What progress have I made that I'm proud of?
- What coping strategies are working effectively for me?
- Which relationships support my healing most effectively?

Areas for Growth:

- What aspects of healing feel most challenging right now?
- Where do I still feel stuck or overwhelmed?
- What patterns or reactions do I want to change?
- What support do I need that I'm not currently receiving?

Healing Goals:

- What does healing look like to me personally?
- How will I know I'm making progress?
- What would I like to feel more capable of handling?
- How do I want to feel about myself and my life?

Inner Child Work Plan

Understanding My Inner Child:

- What messages did my inner child receive about their worth and lovability?
- What did my inner child need that they didn't receive?
- What survival strategies did my inner child develop?
- How do these strategies still show up in my adult life?

Re-parenting Practices:

- How can I provide emotional nurturing to my inner child?
- What boundaries do I need to set to protect my inner child?
- How can I encourage my inner child's authentic self-expression?

- What creative or playful activities would nurture my inner child?

Integration Goals:

- How do I want to integrate my inner child's wisdom with my adult capabilities?
- What aspects of childlike wonder and authenticity do I want to reclaim?
- How can I honor my inner child's needs while maintaining adult responsibilities?

Emotional Regulation Development

Current Regulation Challenges:

- What emotions feel most overwhelming or difficult to manage?
- When do I tend to become emotionally dysregulated?
- What triggers tend to activate my trauma responses?
- How do emotional reactions interfere with my daily life or relationships?

Regulation Skills to Develop:

- What grounding techniques work best for me?
- How can I improve my ability to identify emotions as they arise?
- What self-soothing strategies feel most effective?
- How can I create more emotional safety in my daily life?

Daily Emotional Wellness Plan:

- What morning practices would support emotional regulation?
- How can I check in with my emotions throughout the day?
- What evening practices would help me process daily emotions?
- Who can I turn to when I need emotional support or perspective?

Self-Worth Building Strategy

Identifying Limiting Beliefs:

- What negative beliefs about my worth did I internalize from my family?
- How do these beliefs show up in my current life and relationships?
- What evidence contradicts these negative beliefs about myself?
- What would I believe about my worth if I could choose freely?

Daily Self-Worth Practices:

- How can I speak to myself more compassionately throughout the day?
- What achievements or efforts can I acknowledge more regularly?
- How can I practice internal validation instead of seeking external approval?
- What boundaries would reflect healthy self-respect?

Challenging the Inner Critic:

- What does my inner critic typically say, and whose voice does it sound like?
- How can I recognize and interrupt critical internal dialogue?
- What compassionate responses can I practice when the inner critic becomes active?
- What evidence can I collect that contradicts my inner critic's messages?

Authentic Life Vision

Exploring Authenticity:

- What activities make me feel most alive and energized?
- What values truly matter to me, beyond what I think I should value?
- What dreams or interests did I abandon during my survival-focused years?
- How do I want to contribute meaningfully to the world?

Life Areas for Authentic Expression:

- How might my career or work evolve to better reflect my authentic self?
- What changes do I want to make in my relationships to support authenticity?
- How can I create living spaces that truly reflect my preferences and needs?
- What daily routines would better support my authentic self-expression?

Transition Planning:

- What small steps can I take toward living more authentically?
- What support do I need during periods of significant change?
- How will I handle resistance from others who prefer my old patterns?
- What timeline feels realistic and sustainable for making authentic life changes?

Post-Traumatic Growth Exploration

Identifying Growth Areas:

- How have my difficult experiences contributed to my personal strength?
- What insights about relationships have I gained through my healing journey?
- How has my capacity for empathy and compassion developed?
- What aspects of life do I appreciate more deeply because of my experiences?

Finding Meaning:

- How might my experiences help others who are struggling with similar challenges?
- What generational cycles am I breaking through my healing work?
- How can I use my insights and wisdom to contribute positively to others' lives?
- What creative or meaningful projects might emerge from my healing journey?

Avoiding Gratitude Pressure:

- How can I appreciate my growth without feeling obligated to be grateful for trauma?
- What boundaries do I need around others' expectations about forgiveness or positivity?
- How can I honor both my pain and my progress without minimizing either?

Daily Healing Practices Plan

Morning Practices:

- How will I check in with myself each morning?
- What practices would help me start the day feeling grounded and centered?
- How can I set intentions that support my healing and authenticity?

Throughout the Day:

- What reminders will help me stay connected to my values and boundaries?
- How will I manage stress and emotional activation as it arises?
- What practices can help me stay present and avoid dissociation or overwhelm?

Evening Practices:

- How will I process the day's experiences and emotions?

- What practices help me wind down and prepare for restorative sleep?

- How can I acknowledge my efforts and progress each day?

Weekly and Monthly Practices:

- What regular activities support my ongoing healing and growth?

- How often will I reassess my progress and adjust my healing plan?

- What larger healing goals will I work toward over time?

Support System and Resources

Current Support Assessment:

- Who in my life best understands and supports my healing journey?

- What professional support do I currently have?

- What support groups or communities provide understanding and encouragement?

- What books, podcasts, or other resources contribute to my healing?

Support Needs:

- What additional support would be helpful for my healing journey?

- Where do I need more understanding or encouragement?

- What professional resources might accelerate my progress?

- How can I better utilize the support that's already available?

Community Building:

- How can I contribute support to others who are on similar healing journeys?

- What communities or groups would I like to become more involved with?

- How can I build relationships that support mutual growth and healing?

Emergency and Crisis Planning

Warning Signs:

- What signs indicate I need extra support or professional help?

- How can I recognize when I'm approaching my limits?

- What symptoms suggest I might be sliding into depression, anxiety, or other mental health crises?

Crisis Resources:

- Who can I call during mental health emergencies?

- What professional crisis resources are available to me?

- What strategies have helped me through previous difficult periods?

- How can I prepare my support system to help during crises?

Self-Care Intensification:

- What practices can I increase when I'm struggling?

- How can I adjust my expectations and responsibilities during difficult periods?

- What environments or activities help me feel most grounded during challenges?

Measuring Progress and Celebrating Growth

Progress Indicators:

- How will I recognize when I'm making progress in my healing?

- What specific changes in thoughts, feelings, or behaviors indicate growth?

- How will I track my progress without becoming obsessed with measurement?

Celebration Practices:

- How will I acknowledge and celebrate healing milestones?

- What rituals or practices help me recognize my growth?

- Who will I share my progress with for additional encouragement and validation?

Long-term Vision:

- Where do I hope to be in my healing journey one year from now?

- What kind of life do I want to be living as I continue to heal and grow?

- How do I want to feel about myself and my relationships in the future?

Remember that healing is not a destination but an ongoing journey of growth, self-discovery, and authentic living. Your healing plan should evolve as you do, supporting your continued development while honoring the progress you've already made. Be patient with yourself, celebrate small victories, and trust in your capacity for continued healing and growth.

The most important thing to remember is that you are worth every bit of effort you put into your healing. Every boundary you set, every difficult emotion you process, every moment of self-compassion you practice, all of it contributes to breaking the cycles that harmed you and creating a life that truly reflects your authentic self. Your healing not only transforms your own life but creates positive ripples that will benefit everyone you encounter along the way.

Chapter 15: Your New Beginning

Standing at the end of this journey through the pages of this book, you may feel a complex mix of emotions. Perhaps you feel empowered by the validation and tools you've gained, or maybe you feel overwhelmed by the scope of work ahead. You might feel grieved by the recognition of all you've lost, or hopeful about the life you're beginning to build. All of these feelings are valid, and all are part of the profound transformation that occurs when someone chooses to break free from toxic family patterns and reclaim their authentic life.

This final chapter isn't really an ending; it's a beginning. It's the start of a life lived on your own terms, guided by your own values, and built around relationships that actually nourish and support you. It's the beginning of a legacy you create rather than one you inherited, a story you write rather than one that was imposed upon you.

The journey of breaking toxic family ties is one of the most courageous acts a person can undertake. It requires you to question everything you were taught about love, loyalty, and family. It demands that you prioritize your well-being over others' comfort, your truth over family mythology, and your future over your past. It asks you to believe that you deserve better than what you were given, even when the people who were supposed to love you most told you otherwise.

As we conclude this exploration together, we'll reflect on how far you've come, acknowledge the ongoing nature of healing and growth, and look toward the future with hope and intention. Most importantly, we'll celebrate the incredible strength it took to pick up this book, to question family dynamics that others might never examine, and to begin the work of creating a life that truly reflects who you are meant to be.

Acknowledging How Far You've Come

Before we look ahead to what's possible in your future, it's important to pause and acknowledge the journey you've already taken. The fact that you're reading these words means you've done something remarkable: you've begun to question family dynamics that many people never examine, you've started to prioritize your well-being over family expectations, and you've taken steps toward creating authentic relationships and a life that reflects your true values.

The Courage to Question

Long before you picked up this book, you demonstrated extraordinary courage by questioning family narratives that others around you might accept without examination. Recognizing that your family relationships were toxic required you to trust your own perceptions over the gaslighting and manipulation you may have experienced for years or decades.

This questioning likely came at a cost. You may have faced accusations of being ungrateful, selfish, or disloyal. Other family members might have pressured you to "keep the peace" or "think of the family." Some friends or community members may have struggled to understand your perspective. Despite these pressures, you continued to trust your own experience and work toward healthier relationships.

The ability to see through family mythology and recognize dysfunction for what it is represents a fundamental shift in consciousness. It means you've developed the capacity to think critically about relationships, to trust your own perceptions, and to value your well-being enough to question systems that don't serve you.

The Strength to Set Boundaries

Whether you've implemented no contact, low contact, or other boundary arrangements with toxic family members, you've demonstrated remarkable strength by prioritizing your mental health over family expectations. Setting boundaries with family members requires you to overcome years of conditioning that taught you to put others' needs before your own.

Every time you've said no to a guilt trip, refused to engage with manipulation, or chosen to protect your energy rather than caretake others' emotions, you've strengthened your capacity for self-advocacy. Each boundary you've set has been an act of self-love, even when it felt scary or selfish at the time.

Your boundaries may have evolved over time, and that's completely normal. Perhaps you started with small limits and gradually worked toward stronger boundaries as you built confidence. Or maybe you needed to implement strict no contact immediately for your safety and well-being. Whatever path you've taken, you've learned to trust your own judgment about what you need to feel safe and healthy.

The Wisdom to Build New Relationships

As you've distanced yourself from toxic family relationships, you've likely learned to recognize and cultivate healthier connections. This might involve deepening existing friendships, building chosen family relationships, or simply becoming more selective about who gets access to your time and energy.

Learning to trust your instincts about people, to recognize red flags in new relationships, and to appreciate the people who treat you with genuine respect and care represents profound growth. You've developed discernment about relationships that many people never acquire, and this wisdom will serve you for the rest of your life.

Building new relationships while healing from family trauma requires particular courage because it means making yourself vulnerable again despite past hurts. Every time you've chosen to trust someone new, to share your authentic self, or to invest in a relationship that might flourish, you've demonstrated resilience and hope.

The Commitment to Your Own Healing

Perhaps most importantly, you've made a commitment to your own healing and growth that goes far beyond just escaping toxic relationships. Healing from family trauma is complex work that requires patience, self-compassion, and persistence. It involves not just changing external circumstances but transforming internal patterns of thought, feeling, and behavior.

Your healing journey may have included therapy, support groups, spiritual practices, creative expression, or countless other approaches to processing your experiences and developing new capacities. Each step you've taken toward healing has been an investment in your future self and in the relationships you'll build going forward.

The commitment to healing also means you've learned to reparent yourself; to provide yourself with the nurturing, guidance, and protection you needed but didn't receive. This is profound work that breaks generational cycles and creates new possibilities for how you'll relate to yourself and others.

The Ongoing Nature of Growth

As you move forward from here, it's important to understand that healing and growth are ongoing processes rather than destinations you reach once and for all. There will be setbacks, new challenges, and deeper layers of healing that emerge over time. This isn't a sign of failure; it's the natural progression of human development and recovery.

Healing Isn't Linear

You may find that you revisit issues you thought you'd resolved, or that new life circumstances trigger old patterns or memories. This is completely normal and doesn't mean you're going backward. Healing happens in spirals rather than straight lines. You may circle back to familiar territory but from a higher vantage point with greater wisdom and resources.

Different life stages may bring up new aspects of your family trauma to heal. Having your own children, experiencing the death of parents, or reaching the age your parents were when they harmed you can all trigger new layers of processing and integration. Each of these experiences offers opportunities for deeper healing and understanding.

Growth Requires Ongoing Attention

Just as physical health requires ongoing attention to nutrition, exercise, and medical care, psychological and emotional health requires ongoing attention to your relationships, stress levels, and emotional processing. The skills you've learned for setting boundaries, regulating emotions, and building healthy relationships need practice and refinement over time.

This ongoing attention isn't a burden; it's a gift you give yourself. By continuing to prioritize your mental health and growth, you ensure that you can continue to show up authentically in your relationships and pursue goals that align with your values.

New Challenges Will Arise

As you build a more authentic life, you'll likely encounter new types of challenges that you couldn't have anticipated from your earlier vantage point. Success in your career, deeper intimate relationships, or increased financial stability can all bring new stresses and opportunities for growth.

These challenges aren't setbacks; they're signs that you're living a fuller, more engaged life. The skills you've developed through healing from family trauma will serve you well as you navigate these new territories, and you'll continue to develop new capacities as you encounter new situations.

Celebrating Progress Along the Way

Because healing and growth are ongoing, it's important to regularly acknowledge and celebrate your progress rather than waiting until you feel "completely healed" or "fully recovered." Take time to notice how you handle situations differently now than you did a year ago, how your relationships have improved, or how much more comfortable you've become with setting boundaries.

These celebrations of progress aren't just feel-good exercises; they're important psychological practices that reinforce positive changes and build confidence for future challenges. Keep a record of your growth, whether through journaling, photos, or other documentation that helps you remember how far you've come.

Creating Your Personal Mission Statement

As you move forward into your new beginning, it can be helpful to articulate your personal mission statement, a clear expression of your values, goals, and intentions for how you want to live your life. This mission statement serves as a North Star that guides your decisions and helps you stay aligned with your authentic self.

Identifying Your Core Values

Your core values are the principles that matter most deeply to you, the guidelines that help you determine what's right and wrong, what's worth pursuing, and how you want to treat yourself and others. These values may be very different from what your family of origin valued or what others expect you to prioritize.

Common core values that people discover through healing from toxic family relationships include:

Authenticity: The commitment to being genuine and true to yourself rather than performing roles that others expect you to play.

Emotional safety: Prioritizing relationships and environments where you can be vulnerable without fear of having that vulnerability used against you.

Mutual respect: Insisting on relationships where both people honor each other's autonomy, boundaries, and inherent worth.

Growth and learning: Embracing opportunities for personal development and supporting others' growth rather than trying to keep people stuck in limiting patterns.

Justice and fairness: Working toward conditions where people are treated equitably and harmful behavior has appropriate consequences.

Compassion: Extending kindness and understanding to yourself and others while maintaining appropriate boundaries and expectations.

Creative expression: Honoring your creative impulses and finding ways to contribute beauty, meaning, or innovation to the world.

Community and connection: Building relationships and communities that support mutual flourishing rather than exploitation or competition.

Defining Your Vision for the Future

Beyond identifying your values, creating a personal mission statement involves envisioning what you want your life to look like as you continue to heal and grow. This vision should be inspiring and motivating while also being realistic and achievable.

Consider these areas as you develop your vision.

Relationships: What kinds of relationships do you want to cultivate? How do you want to show up in your friendships, romantic partnerships, and chosen family connections?

Work and contribution: How do you want to contribute to the world through your work, volunteer activities, or creative pursuits? What legacy do you want to create through your efforts?

211

Personal growth: What aspects of yourself do you want to continue developing? What new skills, insights, or capacities would enhance your life and relationships?

Lifestyle: How do you want to structure your daily life to support your well-being and values? What environments, routines, and practices would best support your continued growth?

Community involvement: How do you want to be involved in your community or in causes that matter to you? What change do you want to help create in the world?

Writing Your Mission Statement

Your personal mission statement should be a concise expression of your values and vision that you can refer to when making important decisions. It might be a single paragraph or a series of bullet points—whatever format feels most meaningful and useful to you.

Here's an example of what a personal mission statement might look like:

"My mission is to live authentically, prioritizing my emotional and physical well-being while building relationships based on mutual respect and genuine care. I commit to using my experiences of healing from family trauma to support others on similar journeys, whether through my professional work, volunteer activities, or simply by modeling what healthy boundaries and self-advocacy look like. I will continue growing in my capacity for both self-compassion and accountability, creating a life that reflects my values of justice, creativity, and community connection. I will honor my past experiences without being defined by them, and I will pursue goals that align with my authentic desires rather than reactions to my trauma."

Your mission statement should feel inspiring and true to you. It should capture both who you are now and who you're becoming, serving as a reminder of your commitments to yourself during times when you face difficult decisions or challenges.

Building Your Support Network for the Long Haul

As you continue your journey of healing and authentic living, having a strong support network becomes increasingly important. This network will evolve over time, but investing in relationships that truly support your growth and well-being is one of the most important things you can do for your long-term success.

Types of Support You Need

Emotional support: People who can listen without judgment, offer comfort during difficult times, and celebrate your successes genuinely.

Practical support: People who can help with concrete tasks during busy or challenging periods, everything from helping you move to providing childcare to offering professional references.

Accountability support: People who can help you stay committed to your goals and values, especially when you're tempted to fall back into old patterns.

Growth support: People who encourage your continued development and aren't threatened by your changes or success.

Fun and recreation support: People who help you enjoy life, laugh, and engage in activities that bring you joy and relaxation.

Professional support: Therapists, coaches, spiritual advisors, or other professionals who provide specialized guidance for your continued growth and healing.

Cultivating Mutual Support

The best support networks are based on reciprocity; you both give and receive support from the important people in your life. As you continue to heal and grow stronger, you'll likely find that you have more capacity to support others in their own challenges and growth.

Supporting others isn't only an act of kindness; it can also nurture your own healing. When you help others navigate challenges similar to ones you've faced, you reinforce your own growth and gain additional perspective on your experiences. Supporting others can also provide a sense of meaning and purpose that enhances your overall well-being.

Maintaining Boundaries Even with Supportive People

Even within supportive relationships, maintaining healthy boundaries is important. This might mean:

- Being clear about what types of support you need in different situations
- Saying no to requests for support when you don't have the capacity to help
- Asking for what you need rather than expecting others to guess
- Respecting others' boundaries when they can't provide the support you're seeking
- Maintaining your individual identity and interests within supportive relationships

Growing Your Network Over Time

Your support network will naturally evolve as you grow and change. Some relationships may become closer, while others may become more distant. New people may enter your life who understand and support the person you're becoming in ways that earlier connections couldn't.

Stay open to meeting new people who share your values and interests. This might happen through:

- Professional development activities
- Volunteer work or community involvement
- Classes or workshops related to your interests
- Support groups or therapy groups
- Online communities focused on healing or personal growth
- Spiritual or philosophical communities
- Recreational activities or hobbies

Paying It Forward: How Your Healing Helps Others

One of the most meaningful aspects of healing from family trauma is discovering how your journey can benefit others who are struggling with similar challenges. Your healing doesn't just transform your own life; it has ripple effects that can positively impact your community, future generations, and countless others who need to see that recovery is possible.

Breaking Generational Cycles

Perhaps the most significant way your healing helps others is by breaking generational cycles of trauma and dysfunction. Every toxic pattern you heal in yourself is a pattern that won't be passed on to your children, chosen family members, or others in your influence.

This breaking of cycles might involve:

- Developing healthy communication skills that you model for others
- Learning to regulate emotions in ways that create safety rather than fear
- Establishing boundaries that teach others about respect and healthy relationships
- Processing your own trauma so you don't unconsciously recreate traumatic dynamics
- Building secure attachment relationships that provide new models for connection

The children in your life, whether your own children, nieces and nephews, chosen family children, or children in your community, benefit enormously from having adults who have done their own healing work and can provide safe, consistent, nurturing relationships.

Supporting Others on Similar Journeys

As you heal and grow stronger, you'll likely encounter others who are struggling with toxic family relationships or the aftermath of family trauma. Your presence and example can provide hope and guidance for people who may feel trapped or hopeless about their situations.

This support might take many forms, such as:

Professional work: Many people who heal from family trauma are drawn to careers in counseling, social work, coaching, or other helping professions where they can use their insights to support others.

Volunteer activities: Support groups, crisis hotlines, mentoring programs, and other volunteer opportunities allow you to give back while continuing to process your own experiences.

Informal mentoring: Simply being available to friends, colleagues, or community members who are struggling with family issues can provide invaluable support and perspective.

Creative expression: Writing, art, music, or other creative works that explore themes of healing and recovery can reach people who need to see their experiences reflected and validated.

Advocacy work: Some people find meaning in advocating for policy changes, increased awareness, or improved resources for people dealing with family trauma.

Modeling Healthy Relationships

As you build authentic, healthy relationships in your own life, you provide a model for others of what functional relationships can look like. Many people from toxic families have never seen healthy relationship dynamics up close, so your relationships can serve as examples of what's possible.

This modeling happens naturally as you:

- Communicate directly and honestly in your relationships
- Set and maintain appropriate boundaries
- Handle conflict constructively without attacking or defending
- Support others' growth and autonomy rather than trying to control them
- Express appreciation and affection genuinely

- Take responsibility for your mistakes and make genuine repairs when needed

Contributing to Cultural Change

The work you've done to heal from family trauma and build authentic relationships contributes to larger cultural shifts in how we understand family, trauma, and mental health. Every person who chooses healing over denial, authenticity over performance, and healthy boundaries over toxic loyalty helps create a culture where these choices become more accepted and supported.

Your willingness to talk openly about family dysfunction, to seek therapy or other support, and to prioritize your mental health helps reduce stigma and gives others permission to make similar choices in their own lives.

Maintaining Hope During Difficult Times

As you continue your journey, there will inevitably be difficult periods—times when you feel discouraged about your progress, when old patterns resurface, or when life circumstances create additional stress. During these times, maintaining hope and perspective becomes crucial for continuing to move forward.

Remembering That Setbacks Are Part of the Process

Difficult periods don't mean you're failing or moving backward—they're normal parts of the healing and growth process. Just as physical healing involves some inflammation and discomfort as the body repairs itself, psychological healing involves periods of emotional intensity as you process experiences and develop new capacities.

When you encounter setbacks:

- Remind yourself of how far you've come since you first started this journey
- Review the tools and strategies you've learned that have helped you before
- Reach out to your support network for encouragement and perspective
- Practice extra self-compassion during challenging times
- Look for the lessons or growth opportunities in current difficulties

Keeping a Long-Term Perspective

Day-to-day progress in healing can be difficult to see, but looking back over months or years reveals significant changes. Keep some form of record—whether through journaling, photos, or other documentation—that helps you remember your journey and see your progress over time.

When you're struggling, it can be helpful to remember:

- The person you were before you started this healing work
- Situations you can handle now that once felt overwhelming
- Relationships that have improved through your boundary-setting and growth
- Goals you've achieved that once seemed impossible
- Moments of joy and connection that your healing work has made possible

Finding Support During Dark Times

There may be periods when you feel particularly isolated, discouraged, or over-whelmed by the healing process. During these times, it's especially important to ac-tively seek support rather than trying to tough it out alone.

This support might include:

- Increasing the frequency of therapy sessions or support group attendance
- Reaching out to trusted friends or chosen family members
- Engaging in practices that have helped you feel grounded and connected in the past
- Considering temporary medication support if depression or anxiety becomes severe
- Participating in online communities where others understand your experiences

Remember that seeking help during difficult times is a sign of wisdom and self-care, not weakness or failure.

Celebrating Small Victories

During challenging periods, it becomes even more important to acknowledge and celebrate small victories and progress. These might include:

- Getting through a difficult day without reverting to old coping mechanisms
- Setting a boundary even when you felt scared or guilty
- Asking for help when you needed it
- Choosing self-care over self-sacrifice
- Having a difficult conversation with kindness rather than defensiveness

These small victories accumulate over time to create significant changes in your life and relationships.

Living Your Values Daily

As you move forward into your new beginning, the ultimate test of your healing and growth is how consistently you can live according to your authentic values rather than old patterns of fear, guilt, or people-pleasing. This daily practice of values-based living is what transforms your healing from an abstract concept into a lived reality.

Making Values-Based Decisions

Every day presents opportunities to choose actions that align with your values rather than actions driven by old programming or external pressures. These decisions might involve:

Career choices: Pursuing work that aligns with your values and uses your strengths rather than work that just provides security or external validation.

Relationship decisions: Investing time and energy in relationships that are reciprocal and supportive rather than relationships that require you to hide your authentic self.

Boundary setting: Saying no to requests that don't align with your values or capacity, even when saying yes would be easier or more popular.

Self-care practices: Prioritizing activities that genuinely nourish you rather than activities you think you "should" do or that others expect from you.

Communication styles: Speaking honestly and directly rather than manipulating, people-pleasing, or avoiding difficult conversations.

Financial decisions: Making spending and saving choices that reflect your actual priorities rather than trying to impress others or compensate for feelings of inadequacy.

Navigating Values Conflicts

Sometimes you'll encounter situations where different values conflict with each other, or where living your values creates tension with others' expectations. Learning to navigate these conflicts with integrity is an important part of authentic living.

For example, you might value both honesty and kindness, and find yourself in a situation where being honest might hurt someone's feelings. Or you might value both loyalty and self-preservation, and need to make a choice that protects your well-being even though others see it as disloyal.

In these situations, it's helpful to:

- Consider which value is most important in this particular context
- Look for creative solutions that honor multiple values when possible

- Accept that sometimes you can't please everyone and prioritize your primary values
- Communicate about your values conflicts with trusted advisors
- Remember that living with integrity sometimes requires difficult choices

Building Habits That Support Your Values

Values-based living is supported by daily habits and practices that reinforce your commitments to yourself. These might include:

Morning practices: Starting each day with reflection, meditation, or other activities that connect you with your values and intentions.

Regular check-ins: Periodically assessing whether your actions and choices are aligning with your stated values.

Evening reflection: Ending each day by acknowledging when you lived according to your values and identifying opportunities for better alignment.

Boundary maintenance: Regular practices for maintaining and adjusting your boundaries as needed.

Relationship investment: Deliberately spending time and energy on relationships that support your authentic self.

Self-care routines: Consistent practices that support your physical, emotional, and spiritual well-being.

Growth activities: Engaging in ongoing learning, therapy, or other activities that support your continued development.

Your Ongoing Journey

As we reach the end of this book, it's important to recognize that you're not reaching the end of your journey—you're reaching a new milestone in an ongoing process of healing, growth, and authentic living. The work you've done to break free from toxic family patterns and build healthy relationships is profound and significant, and it will continue to unfold and deepen over time.

Embracing the Unknown

Moving forward from family trauma into authentic living inevitably involves stepping into unknown territory. You're creating a life that's different from what you experienced growing up, and you're building relationships that may be healthier than any you've experienced before. This unknown territory can feel both exciting and frightening.

Embracing the unknown involves:

- Trusting in your capacity to handle challenges as they arise
- Remaining curious about what's possible rather than limiting yourself to what feels familiar
- Being willing to experiment with new ways of being and relating
- Accepting that growth often involves discomfort and uncertainty
- Celebrating the adventure of creating a life that truly reflects your authentic self

Continuing to Learn and Grow

Your healing journey will continue to present new opportunities for learning and growth. You might discover new interests, develop new skills, or encounter new types of relationships that expand your understanding of what's possible. Stay open to these opportunities and remember that learning and growth are lifelong processes.

Some areas where you might continue to grow include:

- Deepening your capacity for intimacy and vulnerability in close relationships
- Developing new professional or creative skills that align with your authentic interests
- Expanding your understanding of trauma, healing, and human development
- Building leadership skills that allow you to support others more effectively
- Exploring spiritual or philosophical questions about meaning and purpose
- Learning to navigate new life stages and transitions with greater wisdom and self-compassion

Trusting Your Inner Wisdom

Perhaps the most important lesson from your journey is learning to trust your own inner wisdom; your intuition, your feelings, your perceptions, and your judgment about what's healthy and right for you. This trust in yourself is the foundation for everything else you've built and will continue to build.

Your inner wisdom has been your guide throughout this process.

- It helped you recognize that something was wrong with your family relationships
- It gave you the courage to question family narratives and set boundaries
- It guided you toward people and resources that supported your healing

- It continues to help you make decisions that align with your authentic self

As you move forward, continue to cultivate and trust this inner wisdom. It will serve you well in navigating future challenges and opportunities.

Gratitude for Your Courage

Finally, take a moment to acknowledge the tremendous courage you've shown throughout this journey. Breaking free from toxic family patterns requires courage that many people never find. Questioning family narratives, setting boundaries with people you love, and building a life based on your authentic self rather than others' expectations, all of this requires extraordinary bravery.

Your courage has not only transformed your own life but has created ripple effects that will benefit countless others. The children in your life will grow up with healthier models of relationships. The friends and colleagues who know you will be inspired by your authenticity and strength. The strangers you encounter will be touched by the compassion and wisdom you've developed through your healing journey.

Reflection: Writing A Letter to Your Future Self

As you complete this book and step into your new beginning, take time to write a letter to your future self. This letter will serve as a reminder of where you are now, what you've learned, and what you hope for as you continue your journey.

Letter to My Future Self

Date: _____

Dear Future Me,

As I write this letter, I am _____ years old and have been working on healing from my family trauma for _____ [time period]. I want you to remember where I am right now in this journey and what I've learned so far.

What I've Overcome

The most significant challenges I've faced and overcome include:

What I've Learned About Myself

Through this healing journey, I've discovered that I am:

The Relationships I've Built

The people who support and nourish me now include:

My Current Values and Priorities

221

The values that guide my decisions now are:

What I'm Most Proud Of

Looking back on my journey, I'm most proud of:

My Hopes for You (Future Me)

As you continue this journey, I hope you will:

Reminders for Difficult Times

When you're struggling, please remember:

- You have survived incredibly difficult circumstances and have the strength to handle whatever comes
- The relationships you've built are evidence of your worth and lovability
- You have tools and resources now that you didn't have before
- Setbacks are part of the process, not evidence of failure
- Your healing benefits not just you but everyone whose life you touch

Questions I Hope You Can Answer

I'm curious about where you'll be when you read this. I wonder:

- How have your relationships continued to deepen and grow?
- What new interests or passions have you discovered?
- How have you been able to use your experiences to help others?
- What unexpected joys has your authentic life brought you?
- What new challenges have you navigated with wisdom and grace?

My Commitment to You

I commit to continuing this healing work not just for who I am now, but for who you will become. I will:

- Keep prioritizing my mental health and well-being
- Continue building relationships based on mutual respect and genuine care
- Stay true to my values even when it's difficult
- Remain open to growth and new experiences
- Practice self-compassion when I make mistakes or face setbacks
- Remember that this journey is worth taking, even when it's hard

Gratitude

I am grateful for:

- The courage to begin this healing journey
- The people who have supported me along the way
- The strength I've discovered within myself
- The possibility of a life lived authentically
- The opportunity to break generational cycles and create something new

Closing Thoughts

As I finish this letter and this book, I feel _____ [describe your current emotional state]. I know that the journey ahead will have both challenges and joys, and I trust that you—my future self—will navigate them with the wisdom and strength we're building together.

I love you, I believe in you, and I'm proud of the courage it takes to live authentically.

With love and hope for our continued journey,

[Your name]

[Today's date]

A Final Word: You Are Worth It

As we close this journey together, I want you to hear one final, crucial message: *You are worth it.*

You are worth the difficulty of setting boundaries with family members who don't understand. You are worth the awkwardness of building new traditions that reflect your actual values. You are worth the courage it takes to trust new people with your authentic self. You are worth the ongoing work of healing, growing, and becoming who you're meant to be.

Your worth isn't conditional on your achievements, your usefulness to others, your ability to keep peace in dysfunctional systems, or your capacity to love people who treat you badly. Your worth is inherent, unchangeable, and absolute. You are worthy of love, respect, safety, and joy simply because you exist.

The toxic family members who couldn't see or celebrate your worth were limited by their own damage and dysfunction. Their inability to value you says nothing about your actual value and everything about their limitations. You don't need their permission to live a beautiful life. You don't need their understanding to know your own truth. You don't need their approval to choose relationships and experiences that nurture your soul.

Your new beginning starts now. It starts with the next choice you make to prioritize your well-being over others' comfort. It continues with the next boundary you set, the next authentic relationship you build, the next moment you choose self-compassion over self-criticism.

The life you're creating, one choice at a time, one day at a time, is a testament to the power of human resilience, the possibility of healing, and the beauty of authentic living. Your journey inspires others who need to see that it's possible to break free from toxic family patterns and create something beautiful in their place.

You have broken the chains that bound you to relationships that diminished you. You have found the courage to step into the unknown territory of authentic living. You are reclaiming your life, your relationships, and your future.

This is your new beginning.

You are worth every bit of work it took to get here.

You are worth every bit of work it will take to continue.

You are worth the beautiful, authentic, meaningful life you're creating.

Welcome to your new beginning. The world is better because you chose to heal, to grow, and to live authentically.

Your journey continues, and it's going to be amazing.